125 Brain Games
for Toddlers and Twos

W9-AUD-033

Other Books by Jackie Silberg

Games to Play With Babies

Games to Play With Toddlers

Games to Play With Two Year Olds

More Games to Play With Toddlers

300 Three Minute Games

500 Five Minute Games

The I Can't Sing Book

125 Brain Games for Babies

Jackie Silberg is an acclaimed speaker, teacher, and trainer on both early childhood development and music. You can arrange to have her speak, present, train, or entertain by contacting her through Gryphon House, PO Box 207, Beltsville MD 20704-0207 or at jsilberg@interserv.com.

125 Brain Games for Toddlers and Twos

for and

simple
games to
promote
early brain
development

Jackie Silberg

Illustrated by Laura D'Argo

gryphon house, inc.

Beltsville, Maryland

DEDICATION

To the wonder and joy of young children

ACKNOWLEDGMENTS

My deepest thanks and appreciation to my editor, Kathy Charner. Your editing is always excellent and encouraging, and your personal warmth is very meaningful to me.

To Leah and Larry Rood, the owners and publishers of Gryphon House, thank you for your wonderful friendship and positive support in all that I do.

Gryphon House books are available at special discount when purchased in bulk for special premiums and sales promotions as well as for fund-raising use. Special editions or book excerpts also can be created to specification. For details, contact the Director of Marketing at the address below.

Copyright © 2000 Jackie Silberg
Published by Gryphon House, Inc.
10726 Tucker Street, Beltsville MD 20705
Visit us on the web at www.gryphonhouse.com

Text Illustration by: Laura D'Argo

Library of Congress Cataloging-in-Publication Data

Silberg, Jackie, 1934-
    125 games for toddlers and twos : simple games to promote early
  brain development/ Jackie Silberg.
        p. cm.
    Includes bibliographical references and index.
    ISBN 0-87659-205-1
    1. Games. 2. Educational games. 3. Toddlers. I. Title: One hundred
  twenty-five games for toddlers and twos. II.Title.

GV1203 . S532 2000

                                                           00-020802

Table of Contents

Introduction

Playing with toddlers and two-year-olds is delightful. These little ones are affectionate, assertive, bouncy, challenging, curious, enchanting, energetic, funny, independent, joyful, lovable, nosey, observant, precious, self-confident, squirmy, surprising, and unpredictable.

This book is about helping to "grow" the brain of these lovely human beings by playing meaningful games with them. Whether it's through singing, dancing, cuddling, rocking, talking, smelling, or tasting, you can encourage the pathways of the brain to make new connections.

By the time a child is three, her brain has formed about 1000 trillion connections—about twice as many as adults have. A baby's brain is superdense, and will stay that way throughout the first decade of life. Beginning at about age eleven, a child's brain gets rid of extra connections, gradually making order out of a thick tangle of "wires."

Some brain cells, called neurons, are hard-wired to other cells before birth. They control the heartbeat, breathing, and reflexes, and regulate other functions essential to survival. The rest of the brain connections are just waiting to be "hooked up." Brain cells are entirely planned for making connections. Each cell sends signals out to other brain cells and receives input from other cells. The signals, in the form of electrical impulses, travel down the length of the nerve cell. Certain chemicals (such as serotonin) travel from cell to cell, creating connections. A single cell can connect with as many as 15,000 other cells. The incredibly complex network of connections that results is often referred to as the brain's "wiring" or "circuitry." The connections neurons make with one another are called synapses. The receptive branches of the nerve cells, called dendrites, are growing and reaching out to form trillions upon trillions of synapses. The brain's weight triples to nearly adult size. While various parts of the brain develop at different rates, study after study has shown that the peak production period for synapses is from birth to about age ten.

How does the brain know which connections to keep? This is where early experience comes into play. Through repetition, brain connections become permanent. Conversely, a connection that is not used at all, or often enough, is unlikely to survive. Chances are a child submerged in language from birth will learn to speak very well. A child whose coos are met with smiles, rather than apathy, will likely become emotionally responsive. A child who is rarely spoken to or read to in the early years may have difficulty mastering language skills later on. A child who is rarely played with may have difficulty later on with social adjustment. "The child who learns piano will learn those connections and, 20 years later, will learn to play again easier than someone who has not studied it," says Harry Chugani, a neuroscientist at Children's Hospital and Wayne State University in Detroit. The synapses that are not used repeatedly will die off while others will remain.

Scientists have learned more in the past ten years about how the human brain works than in all of previous history, and their knowledge is doubling every ten years! Their recent discovery that early childhood experiences profoundly shape the infant brain is changing the way we think about the needs of children. The research also supports the long-held beliefs that an individual's capacity to learn and thrive in a variety of settings depends on the interplay between nature (their genetic endowment) and nurture (the kind of care, stimulation, and teaching they receive); that the human brain is uniquely constructed to benefit from experience and from good teaching, particularly during the first years of life; and that, while the opportunities and risks are greatest during the first years of life, learning takes place throughout the human life cycle.

The very best way to develop young children's brain connections is to give children what they need, which is an environment that is interesting to explore, that is safe, and that is filled with people who will respond to their emotional and intellectual needs. Brain research supports what we already know: Young children need loving, supportive people in their lives who will sing to them, hug them, talk to them, read to them, not flash cards in their faces. All the games in this book develop the brain capacity of toddlers and two-year-olds. They are the building blocks for future learning—a good, solid beginning for little ones and enjoyable at the same time. Each game in the book refers to related brain research. We can help children grow and learn by asking them meaningful questions; by exposing them to a variety of experiences, activities, and toys; and, of course, by giving them love and security.

> If you touch me soft and gentle,
> If you look at me and smile,
> If you talk to me and listen,
> I will grow, really grow.
> Anonymous

The Pushing Game

WHAT BRAIN RESEARCH SAYS

If the brain's neurons that are connected with sight and motor skills are not trained at an early age, by adulthood they will simply not be "plastic" enough to be rewired for many experiences.

■ Toddlers love to push things. They enjoy watching the movement and knowing that they have made the object move.

■ Pushing games make a young child feel powerful and in control. They are a wonderful way to develop a toddler's confidence and coordination.

■ Select several items for your child to push. Choose very lightweight objects such as a stuffed animal, a small toy, or a push toy.

■ Say, "One, two, three, push," and then push one of the toys.

■ Repeat the counting and encourage your child to do the pushing.

■ When your little one keeps saying "tree" (meaning the word "three") all day long, you will know that she loves this game!

2

WHAT BRAIN RESEARCH SAYS

According to Dr. Bruce Perry, a psychiatrist at Baylor College of Medicine, children who don't get their quota of TLC early in life may lack the proper wiring to form close relationships.

Lots of TLC

- This game develops nurturing skills.

- Sit on the floor with your toddler and put two or three of your toddler's favorite stuffed animals on the floor with you.

- Pick up one of the stuffed toys and cuddle it in your arms. Say loving words like, "Playing with you is so much fun," "I love your brown fur," or "I love to hug you."

- Now do the same thing to your child.

- Give your child one of the animals and ask her to cuddle it and give it kisses.

- Keep the game going as long as your toddler is interested. You will soon notice that your toddler will be playing the game by herself.

Practicing Parentese

3

WHAT BRAIN RESEARCH SAYS

Because young children pay close attention to the high-pitched, singsong speech known as "parentese," they will learn the importance of words.

- The word "parentese" means to speak and sing to your child in a high-pitched voice.

- Practice singing some of your favorite songs like "Twinkle, Twinkle Little Star," "Do you Know the Muffin Man?" or "I've Been Working on the Railroad" in a parentese voice.

- Hold your child close to you and sing the songs two ways—first, the regular way and second, the parentese way.

- Your toddler will pay particular attention to the second time you sing.

Crawl to the Toy

WHAT BRAIN RESEARCH SAYS

Minerals in the body are the raw materials necessary for building brain connections. One reason some children learn to crawl and walk earlier than others is that they produce minerals earlier in their development.

■ When your toddler is crawling, encourage this movement with the following game.

■ Place a favorite toy at one end of the room.

■ Get down on the floor and crawl to the toy. When you reach the toy, pick it up and pretend that it says, "Come on (child's name), can you come get me?"

■ Encourage your little one to crawl to the toy.

■ If your child is getting ready to walk, place the toy at a higher level so that she will try to pull herself up to reach it.

■ It's also a lot of fun to crawl around in a circle with your child.

1, 2, 3, Bump

5

WHAT BRAIN RESEARCH SAYS

Touch stimulates the brain to release important hormones that allow your child to grow. Your love is the key to the powerful connection between the two of you, but the expression of your love affects the way her brain forms connections.

- Sit your toddler on your lap facing you.

- Say, "One, two, three, bump." On the word "bump," hold her head and bump it very gently against yours.

- Say the words again and this time gently bump noses on the word "bump."

- Continue the game, gently bumping different parts of the body such as elbows, knees, cheeks, ears, and chins.

Recent studies have shown how exposure to music affects spatial-temporal reasoning—the ability to see a disassembled picture and mentally piece it back together. Such reasoning underlies math, engineering, and other disciplines.

Rock-a-bye Baby

■ Hold your child in your arms and rock her back and forth as you sing lullabies and other soothing songs, such as the following.

- "Goodnight, Irene"

- "Hush Little Baby" (The Mockingbird Song)

- "Kumbaya"

- "Rock-a-bye Baby"

- "Swing Low, Sweet Chariot"

■ Use a rocking motion to calm your child and develop trust between the two of you.

■ After the last line of the song, hold your toddler close and give her a big hug.

Peekaboo Games

WHAT BRAIN RESEARCH SAYS

With every game of peekaboo, thousands of connections among brain cells are formed or strengthened, adding a bit more definition and complexity to the intricate circuitry that will remain largely in place for the rest of the child's life.

■ Peekaboo is not only fun for your toddler, it is also very important for "growing" the brain.

■ You can play peekaboo by...

- covering your eyes with your hands.

- putting a towel over your face.

- hiding behind a door or large piece of furniture and popping out.

- putting your toddler's hands over her eyes and then taking them away.

- placing a toy or stuffed animal under a cover and pulling the cover away.

- drawing a face on your thumb with a marker and hiding your thumb under your other fingers.

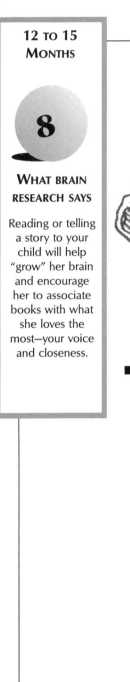

8

Reading or telling a story to your child will help "grow" her brain and encourage her to associate books with what she loves the most—your voice and closeness.

Reading Games

■ There are many ways you can help your toddler develop a love of reading, including the following.

- Encourage your toddler to play with books such as *Pat the Bunny,* Dorothy Kunhardt's classic touch-and-feel book, and cloth or sturdy cardboard books.

- Point to pictures in books and name the various objects.

- Sing the nursery rhymes in books.

- Vary the tone of your voice, make funny faces, or do other special effects when you read to stimulate your child's interest in books and stories.

- Read to your toddler often, but for short periods of time.

Yum, Yum

WHAT BRAIN RESEARCH SAYS

Tone and facial expressions are understood before words. Emotional learning is intertwined with all domains of learning.

- Develop your toddler's language skills when you prepare a meal or snack by chanting the following verse or singing it to the tune of "The Farmer in the Dell."

> *It's time to find the milk*
> *It's time to find the milk*
> *Hi, ho, the derry oh*
> *It's time to find the milk.*

- Walk to the refrigerator and take out the milk carton. Say, "Oh boy, I love milk. Yum, yum."

- Use the chant with other foods or household items. Take out the item, chant the verse, then talk about the food.

- Expressing pleasant emotions with your toddler is very good for brain development.

- In addition, games such as this one develop language skills.

10

WHAT BRAIN RESEARCH SAYS

For a young child's brain to grow and thrive, the child needs to be loved, held, talked to, read to, and allowed to explore.

Song Patting

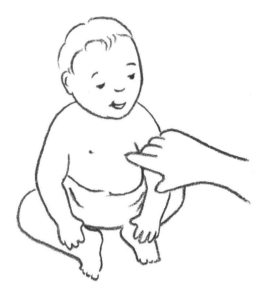

- Try song patting when changing a diaper, giving your toddler a bath, or any time.

- Sing your favorite song to your toddler and, at the same time, pat her tummy or back with your index finger to the rhythm of the song.

- Always end the song with a snuggly kiss.

- You can also sing one line of the song and pat only one word. For example, "Twinkle, twinkle, little (pat the word "star" but don't sing it)."

- This game helps develop a child's sense of rhythm and her listening skills.

Bouncing, Bouncing

11

WHAT BRAIN RESEARCH SAYS

Positive interactions with caring adults stimulate a child's brain, causing synapses to grow and existing connections to be strengthened.

- This enjoyable bouncing game is a great bonding experience for you and your toddler.

- Put your child on your lap facing you. Hold her firmly under the arms.

- Say the following as you bounce your child on your lap.

> *Bouncing, bouncing, let's go bouncing.*
> *Up and down,*
> *All around.*
> *Bouncing, bouncing, let's go bouncing.*
> *Whoops, don't fall down. (tip your toddler to one side)*

- Say the poem again and "tip" to the other side.

- Repeat the poem and on the word "whoops" open up your knees while holding your toddler firmly and let her fall back.

Children who have loving, consistent, sensitive caretakers will have social and cognitive skills in childhood that are superior to those of children who did not benefit from such care.

Go to Bed Late

■ Hold your toddler in your lap and say the following rhyme. Hold her hands up high in the air for the word "tall" and down to her toes for the word "small."

> *Go to bed late,*
> *You will stay very small.*
> *Go to bed early,*
> *You will grow very tall.*

■ You can also hold her while you are standing. This time hold her high in the air for the word "tall" and down to the ground for the word "small."

■ Doing things with your toddler that you both enjoy will form a strong bond between you.

The Singsong Game

13

Talking to a young child increases the number of words that she will recognize and eventually understand. She also will learn better when occasionally spoken to in singsong tones.

- This delightful game enhances a child's language skills.

- Instead of speaking words in your regular voice, try using a singsong voice; make your voice sing the sounds of the words upward and then downward.

- The famous "naa naa naa naa naa naa" to the same melody as "Ring Around the Rosy" is a singsong sound.

- Sing sentences like "Let's go play with blocks" or "I am going to tickle you."

- Sit on the floor with your toddler and put one of her favorite stuffed toys in your lap. Sing to the toy in your singsong voice and then give the toy to your little one.

- If she tries to copy you, you will soon hear your toddler playing the same game when she is by herself.

WHAT BRAIN RESEARCH SAYS

Small muscle exercises stimulate brain growth. Researchers have verified the positive effects of finger and hand movements on the brain.

Jack in the Box

■ This game develops fine motor skills.

■ Say the following rhyme and do the accompanying motions.

> *Jack in the box, Jack in the box (make a fist with your right hand and hide your thumb inside)*
>
> *It's time to wake up and smile. (knock on your fist with your other hand)*
>
> *One, two, three, four (keep knocking)*
>
> *Out Jack pops from his little round door. (pop your thumb out from inside your fist.)*

■ Repeat the poem and encourage your toddler to do the actions with you.

Good Sounds, Bad Sounds

WHAT BRAIN RESEARCH SAYS

Emotional stability is greatly affected by how the brain develops in the first two years of life.

- Toddlers may become frightened by certain sounds.

- Helping your toddler become aware of sounds may reassure her that sounds are good.

- Listen to a clock and see if you can copy the sound.

- Go from room to room and listen for sounds. Listen to a heat register, to an icemaker, or to a radio playing.

- You can also create sounds by opening and closing a door, a window, or a drawer.

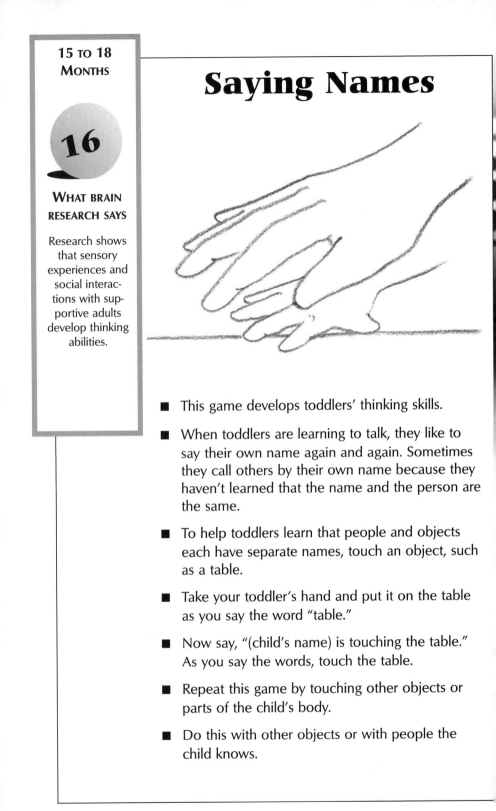

What brain research says

Research shows that sensory experiences and social interactions with supportive adults develop thinking abilities.

Saying Names

- This game develops toddlers' thinking skills.

- When toddlers are learning to talk, they like to say their own name again and again. Sometimes they call others by their own name because they haven't learned that the name and the person are the same.

- To help toddlers learn that people and objects each have separate names, touch an object, such as a table.

- Take your toddler's hand and put it on the table as you say the word "table."

- Now say, "(child's name) is touching the table." As you say the words, touch the table.

- Repeat this game by touching other objects or parts of the child's body.

- Do this with other objects or with people the child knows.

Early Block Fun

WHAT BRAIN RESEARCH SAYS

Although fine and gross motor skills require the same physical foundations, they develop separately. If a child is putting lots of effort into gross motor skills one week, he won't be working much on fine motor skills at the same time.

- Make disposable blocks out of small milk cartons.

- Tape all of the ends together and cover the cartons with contact paper.

- Encourage your toddler to decorate the blocks with crayons or stickers.

- Play a stacking game with your toddler. Praise him each time he stacks one block on top of another.

- Sometimes your toddler may have more fun knocking down the stacks.

- The great thing about these blocks is that you can throw them away when they get worn out.

- Decorating these blocks and stacking them help develop fine motor skills.

WHAT BRAIN RESEARCH SAYS

A child's brain thrives on feedback from its environment. It "wires" itself into a thinking and emotional organ based on its experiences.

Follow the Leader

- By encouraging your toddler to copy you as you do different activities, you help him develop his observation and listening skills.

- If your little one is crawling, you can crawl to different parts of a room and do silly activities.

- If your toddler is walking, you can do the same activities by walking or combining walking and crawling.

- Describe what you are doing. For example, "I am walking (or crawling) slowly around the chair."

- Here are a few ideas.

  - Crawl or walk to the wall and say "ta dah!"

  - Crawl or walk to the door and count to three.

  - Walk in a circle and sit down saying, "chi, chi, boom!"

Sing Out

WHAT BRAIN RESEARCH SAYS

The earlier a child is introduced to music, the more potential he has for learning and enjoying music.

■ Enjoy singing with your toddler any time during the day—while you are in the car, waiting in line at the supermarket, or sitting in a doctor's office. Any time is a good time to sing.

■ Develop your child's musical abilities and sensibilities by singing to him. Don't worry about singing in key or changing the words of a song. Enjoying the singing is the important part. The following are some suggestions for songs, although any song you know and love would be fine.

- "If You're Happy and You Know It"
- "I'm a Little Teapot"
- "Going to the Zoo"
- "Five Little Ducks"
- "The Itsy Bitsy Spider"
- "On Top of Spaghetti"
- "This Old Man"
- "Skip to My Lou"

20

Story Time

■ This game develops a toddler's pre-reading skills and encourages him to love books and reading.

■ Reading books to toddlers can be frustrating. It's important to realize that two to four minutes is about as long as your little one can sit still.

■ Toddlers are interested in books with photos of children doing familiar things like eating, running, and sleeping.

■ Books about saying "hello" and "good-bye" are popular with this age child.

■ Simple rhymes and predictable text are also important criteria for a toddler book.

■ To increase your child's interest in a book, substitute your child's name for the name of a child in the book.

■ You can read anywhere—on a bed, at bath time (using waterproof books, of course), sitting on the floor, in a swing.

Playing With Texture

WHAT BRAIN RESEARCH SAYS

Children who grow up in an environment rich in language are almost always fluent by age three. People deprived of language as children rarely master it as adults, no matter how smart they are or how intensively they're trained.

- This game develops tactile awareness and language skills.

- Put together several objects with interesting textures for your toddler to experience, such as something hard (a block) and something soft (a squishy toy).

- Put his hand on a hard item you have chosen and say the name of the item with the word "hard" before it. "Hard block." Now put his hand on something else that is hard and say the name again. "Hard table."

- Do this several times before you introduce the soft items, such as a soft rug or a soft pillow.

- When you say the word "hard" use a hard sounding voice, and when you say the word "soft" use a soft voice.

WHAT BRAIN RESEARCH SAYS

Young children fall in love with their parents. Psychologists call it "attachment." First postulated by British psychiatrist John Bowlby in the 1950s, attachment remains one of this century's more enduring theories of human development.

The Cuddle Game

■ Cuddling your toddler is a very important way to build his brain capacity.

■ In times of danger, cuddling is even more important.

■ If your little one wanders where he is not allowed to go, pick him up and cuddle him while explaining, "You cannot go there because it is dangerous."

■ He will understand by the tone of your voice that what he did is a "no-no."

■ By the way that you hold him as you say those words, he will also understand that you care and want to protect him.

■ This engenders the development of trust.

Nighttime Is Special

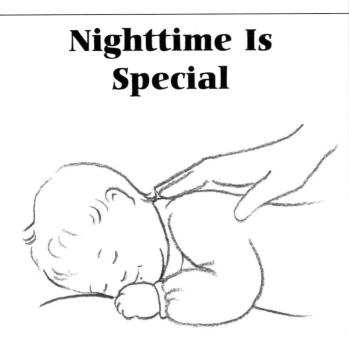

23

WHAT BRAIN RESEARCH SAYS

Young children and their parents are biologically "wired" to forge a close emotional tie, which develops slowly over the baby's first years of life through an ongoing dialogue of coos, gazes, and smiles.

- Establishing a bedtime routine for your toddler is very important. It gives him a sense of trust and stability.

- Back rubbing and singing are nice ways to relax your energetic toddler, who has been running and jumping all day.

- Sing the following to the tune of "Are You Sleeping." Rub your child's back at the same time.

> *Good night, Sammy*
> *Good night, Sammy*
> *Go to sleep, go to sleep.*
> *Soon you will be dreaming.*
> *Soon you will be dreaming.*
> *I love you, I love you.*

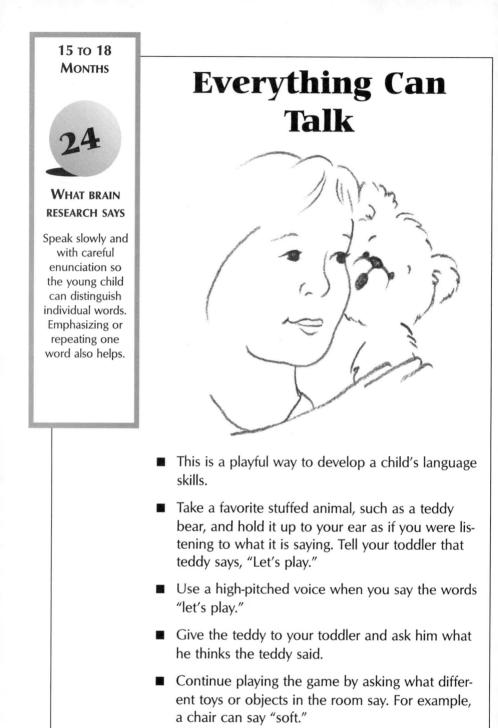

24

What brain research says

Speak slowly and with careful enunciation so the young child can distinguish individual words. Emphasizing or repeating one word also helps.

Everything Can Talk

- This is a playful way to develop a child's language skills.

- Take a favorite stuffed animal, such as a teddy bear, and hold it up to your ear as if you were listening to what it is saying. Tell your toddler that teddy says, "Let's play."

- Use a high-pitched voice when you say the words "let's play."

- Give the teddy to your toddler and ask him what he thinks the teddy said.

- Continue playing the game by asking what different toys or objects in the room say. For example, a chair can say "soft."

- Always use a high-pitched voice when speaking for the toy or object.

At the Garden Gate

WHAT BRAIN RESEARCH SAYS

A strong, secure attachment to a nurturing adult (bonding) can have a protective function, helping a growing child withstand the ordinary stresses of daily life.

- Sit your toddler in your lap.

- Take his hand in yours and show him how to close his fingers and make a fist.

- Say the following rhyme as you gently tap on your child's fist with your finger.

> Jasper's at the garden gate. (use your child's name)
>
> Jasper's at the garden gate.
>
> Jasper's at the garden gate.
>
> Open the door and let him in. (show your child how to open his fist)

- When the fist is open, take your fingers and tickle the palm of his hand and kiss his fingers.

- Keep repeating the game and soon he will open his fist when he hears the word "open."

26

What brain research says

Every new move has to be repeated over and over to strengthen neural circuits that wind from the brain's thinking areas into the motor cortex and out to nerves connected to muscles.

Rolling Fun

- Your toddler has reached the age where rolling balls is fun to do.

- You can develop his motor skills by rolling a ball to him and encouraging him to roll it back.

- Sit on the floor with your child. Call out his name so he will look at you, then roll the ball to him.

- Encourage him to roll it back to you.

- As you are rolling, chant the words "I roll the ball to (child's name)."

- When he rolls the ball back to you, chant "(child's name) rolls the ball to (daddy)."

- Only chant the words when the actual rolling is taking place.

Chook, Chook

WHAT BRAIN RESEARCH SAYS

Small muscle exercises like finger-plays stimulate brain growth. Researchers have verified the positive effects of moving fingers and hands on the brain.

■ This is a wonderful fingerplay game that will develop your child's fine motor skills and provide fun for both of you.

■ Sit your toddler in your lap and move his fingers to fit the rhyme.

Chook, chook (speak like a chicken)

Chook, chook, chook

Good morning, Mrs. Hen.

How many chickens have you got?

Madam, I've got ten. (hold up child's 10 fingers)

Four of them are yellow (put down four fingers on one hand, keep the thumb up)

And four of them are brown (put down four fingers on the other hand, keep the thumb up)

And two of them are speckled red (touch thumb of each hand)

The nicest in the town. (kiss child's two thumbs)

**WHAT BRAIN
RESEARCH SAYS**

Exposure to a
variety of musical
stimuli and
sounds, stimu-
lates and devel-
ops listening skills
in the early years
of a child's devel-
opment.

Toy Sounds

■ Think about the toys that your toddler likes to
  play with and encourage him to make up sounds
  that the toys could make.

  • Trains—train sound

  • Cars—car sounds

  • Stuffed animals—make up voices

  • Dolls—make up voices

  • Blocks—the taller the tower, the higher the
    voice

Going to the Park

29

WHAT BRAIN RESEARCH SAYS

Helping a child's brain "grow" means immersing him in environments that are rich and stimulating, both emotionally and intellectually.

■ This game develops toddlers' language skills.

■ Toddlers love their stuffed toys, and you will often hear them carrying on a conversation with a stuffed animal.

■ Engage your little one in a pretend game of "Going to the Park" with his stuffed toys.

■ Ask questions that encourage him to talk. For example, "What do you think teddy should wear today?" "Is it cold outside?" "If teddy doesn't wear shoes, what will happen to his feet?"

■ More ideas for questions are "What shall we take to the park for lunch?" or "What does your monkey like to eat?"

■ Always respond to what your child says, which will encourage him to talk even more.

■ Language skills are also essential when a toddler is older and learning to read.

30

What brain research says

When a child hears the sounds of a language, neural links are formed in the brain that will allow the child to build a vocabulary of a language.

Bon Jour and Buenos Dias

■ Your toddler is at the perfect age for exposure to the sounds of other languages.

■ If you speak two languages, talk to your toddler in both. Even if you speak only English, try saying "hello" in different languages.

> *Hola (o-la)—Spanish*
>
> *Ciao (chow) —Italian*
>
> *Moshi (mo-she) —Japanese*
>
> *Jambo (jom-bow) —African*
>
> *Shalom (sha-lome) —Israeli*
>
> *Yasoo (ya-zoo) —Greek*

■ Listen to songs in another language. You will be amazed how quickly your child will pick them up. Even if he isn't saying the words, his brain is sending all the right signals for this language to be retained.

■ Read stories that incorporate other languages besides your own native tongue.

One Little Foot, I Love You

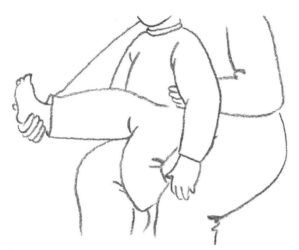

WHAT BRAIN RESEARCH SAYS

Adults can foster a toddler's sunny disposition with smiles and animated enthusiasm. The way a child feels about himself and the world is reflected in his relationship with his primary caregiver.

■ Sit on the floor with your toddler in your lap.

■ Lift up one of his feet and say the following poem.

> *One little foot, I love you.*
>
> *One little foot, I love you.*
>
> *Shake it to the left. (move your toddler's foot to the left)*
>
> *Shake it to the right. (move your toddler's foot to the right)*
>
> *One little foot, I love you.*

■ Kiss your toddler's foot.

■ Repeat the poem for as long as your child will sit still. Say the poem about different parts of the body.

> *One little hand...*
>
> *One little finger...*
>
> *One little head...*

32

WHAT BRAIN RESEARCH SAYS

The brain has a boundless capacity to store information. Each time it processes new information, it goes through physical and chemical changes that form neural networks.

The Cow Says Moo

- Toddlers enjoy learning animal sounds. This also helps them develop beginning speech.

- Toddlers need to say as many sounds as they can. The more they talk, the more they will want to talk.

- Look through animal picture books and talk about the sounds that the animals make.

- Make an animal sound that your child will recognize and ask him to show you a picture in the book of the animal that makes that sound.

- Add sounds to your repertoire—a car sound, a fire engine sound, bird sounds, etc.

- Help your child become aware of the sounds around him.

Looking at Me

33

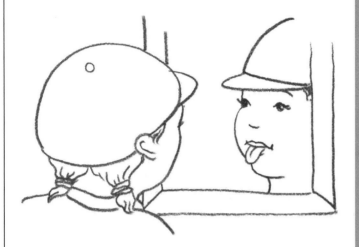

WHAT BRAIN RESEARCH SAYS

Sensory experiences and social interactions with supportive adults help the child develop thinking abilities.

■ Look into a mirror with your toddler and let her watch her face as she does different things.

■ As she watches herself in the mirror, ask her to do the following.

- Smile.

- Stick out her tongue and inspect it.

- Open and close her mouth.

- Look at her teeth.

■ Give her something to eat and let her watch herself chew (with her mouth closed, of course!).

■ This game helps her become more aware of herself and her abilities.

34

WHAT BRAIN RESEARCH SAYS

Exercising forms and strengthens neural bridges that are necessary for learning academic skills later in life.

Cat and Mouse

- Tell your toddler that you are a tiny little mouse and that she is a cat that is going to chase you.

- Tell her that the mouse says, "Squeak, squeak," and the cat says, "Meow, meow."

- Get down on the floor and say, "You can't catch me!" Start crawling quickly and encourage your child to chase you.

- Crawl behind furniture, under tables, and into other rooms.

- When your child understands the game, switch parts.

- This is a wonderful way to develop large motor muscles.

Tops and Bottoms

WHAT BRAIN RESEARCH SAYS

Teaching concepts such as top and bottom nurtures connections that develop the capacity of the brain.

- Sit on the floor with your toddler.

- Take three or four blocks and build a tower.

- Take a toy and put it on top of the blocks and say, "The toy is on the top."

- Knock the toy off the top of the tower and say, "The toy is on the bottom."

- Repeat the game, letting your toddler move the toy from top to bottom.

**WHAT BRAIN
RESEARCH SAYS**

Early childhood
experiences have
a dramatic
impact, physically
determining how
the intricate neu-
ral circuits of the
brain are "wired."

Different Voices

■ Talking and singing in different voices is a good
way to encourage language development.

■ Sing a simple song that you know.

■ First sing it in a normal singing voice.

■ Now change your voice and try to get your
toddler to do the same. Try different voices,
including

• High voice

• Low voice

• Soft voice

• Nasal voice (hold your nose as you sing)

■ This kind of game will help your young child
learn about patterns of speech.

An Imaginary Friend

WHAT BRAIN RESEARCH SAYS

The young brain grows phenomenally in the first years of life, opening windows of opportunity for learning that occurs only once in a lifetime.

- Take a paper cup and cut a small circle out of the side.

- The hole should be big enough for you to put your finger through. Your finger will become the nose on the puppet.

- Draw eyes and a smiling mouth around the hole.

- Talk to your toddler with the puppet and tell her positive things about herself.

- Say things like "I like you" or "You have a nice smile."

- Ask her questions that she can respond to and then praise her answers.

**WHAT BRAIN
RESEARCH SAYS**

Children learn a
language by hear-
ing words over
and over. That's
why the earlier
you start talking
to children the
better.

Words, Words, Words

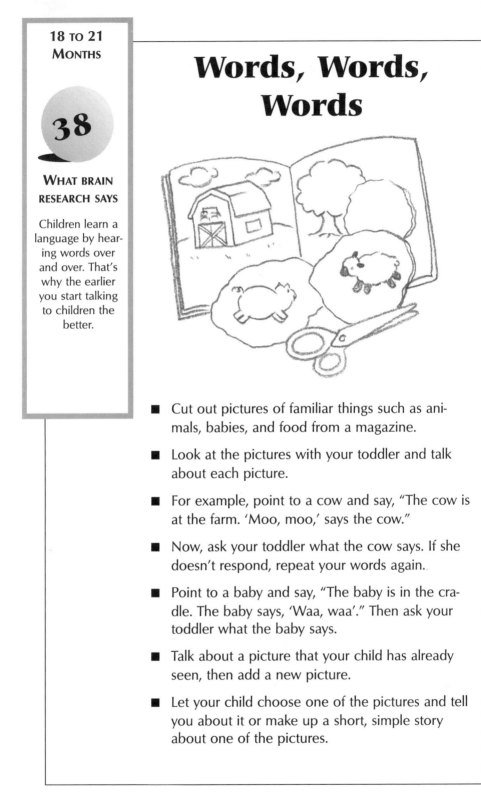

- Cut out pictures of familiar things such as animals, babies, and food from a magazine.

- Look at the pictures with your toddler and talk about each picture.

- For example, point to a cow and say, "The cow is at the farm. 'Moo, moo,' says the cow."

- Now, ask your toddler what the cow says. If she doesn't respond, repeat your words again.

- Point to a baby and say, "The baby is in the cradle. The baby says, 'Waa, waa'." Then ask your toddler what the baby says.

- Talk about a picture that your child has already seen, then add a new picture.

- Let your child choose one of the pictures and tell you about it or make up a short, simple story about one of the pictures.

Someone Special

WHAT BRAIN RESEARCH SAYS

When children have a nurturing environment early in life, they often have higher IQ scores and adjust more easily to school.

■ Develop your toddler's listening skill by saying the following poem to her.

> *I know someone very special.*
> *Do you know who?*
> *I'll turn around and turn around. (turn around)*
> *And then I'll point to you! (point to your child)*
>> *Jackie Silberg*

■ Ask your child to turn around as you say the poem.

■ Repeat the poem and change the action. Instead of turning around, you can jump up and down, clap your hands, fly like a bird, etc.

■ This game develops your child's listening skills because she must listen to know what to do.

WHAT BRAIN RESEARCH SAYS

Early experiences are critical. If you provide the same type of experiences for the same period of time when a child is ten, they will not have the same impact as they would for a child who is one or two.

Let's Talk

■ Talking to your toddler develops her language skills.

■ Choose subject matter that she is interested in. It might be about her toys, grandparents, or pets.

■ Add descriptive words as you talk about a particular subject. For example, say, "I like this bunny rabbit. He feels soft and cuddly."

■ As you say these words, cuddle the toy and stroke it.

■ Give the bunny rabbit to your toddler. Repeat the words and encourage her to cuddle and stroke it.

■ The words "soft" and "cuddly" can apply to other toys.

■ Soon these descriptive words will become a part of your toddler's vocabulary.

Let's Sing

WHAT BRAIN RESEARCH SAYS

Musical games often combine rhythmic movement with speech or singing. The brain cells that control these activities also regulate motor impulses, so these activities develop a child's ability to control her movements.

■ Dolls and stuffed animals are very special friends to toddlers.

■ Singing with a stuffed animal will help develop your child's language.

■ Take a stuffed animal and put it in your lap.

■ Sing a song, any song, and make up actions to go with it. Here are some suggested songs and examples of actions to include.

> *"Pop Goes the Weasel"—on the word "pop" take a stuffed animal and hold it high in the air.*

> *"Heads, Shoulders, Knees, and Toes"—point to each part of the stuffed animal's body as it is named in the song.*

> *"If You're Happy and You Know it"—clap stuffed animal's hands at the end of the line of the song.*

■ Give the stuffed animal to your toddler and help her do the actions with the stuffed animal while you sing the song.

42

WHAT BRAIN RESEARCH SAYS

At no other stage does the brain master so many activities with such ease. At no other time do experiences affect us so deeply.

Lots of Movement

■ To develop your toddler's motor skills, sing the following to the tune of "London Bridge Is Falling Down" and follow the directions.

> *Put your hands up in the air,*
> *In the air, in the air.*
> *Put your hands up in the air,*
> *Clap, clap, clap.*

> *Put your hands down to the ground,*
> *To the ground, to the ground.*
> *Put your hands down to the ground,*
> *Clap, clap, clap.*

■ Additional ideas include

> *Kick your leg into the air...*
> *Move your arm from side to side...*
> *Take your legs and march, march, march...*

The Classics

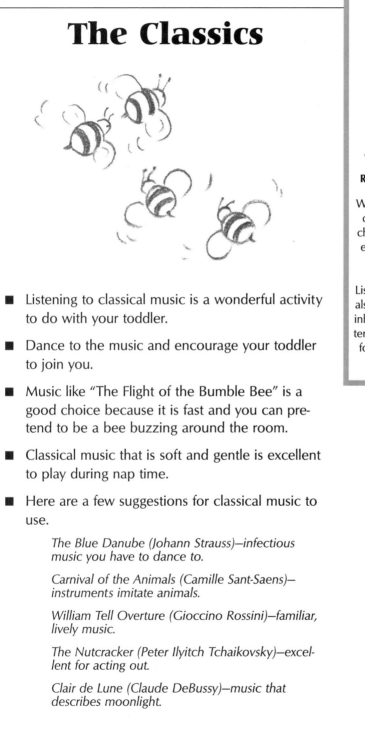

**WHAT BRAIN
RESEARCH SAYS**

When listening to
classical music,
children strength-
en the brain cir-
cuits used for
mathematics.
Listening to music
also enhances the
inherent brain pat-
terns that are used
for complex rea-
soning tasks.

■ Listening to classical music is a wonderful activity
to do with your toddler.

■ Dance to the music and encourage your toddler
to join you.

■ Music like "The Flight of the Bumble Bee" is a
good choice because it is fast and you can pretend to be a bee buzzing around the room.

■ Classical music that is soft and gentle is excellent
to play during nap time.

■ Here are a few suggestions for classical music to
use.

> *The Blue Danube (Johann Strauss)–infectious
> music you have to dance to.*

> *Carnival of the Animals (Camille Sant-Saens)–
> instruments imitate animals.*

> *William Tell Overture (Gioccino Rossini)–familiar,
> lively music.*

> *The Nutcracker (Peter Ilyitch Tchaikovsky)–excel-
> lent for acting out.*

> *Clair de Lune (Claude DeBussy)–music that
> describes moonlight.*

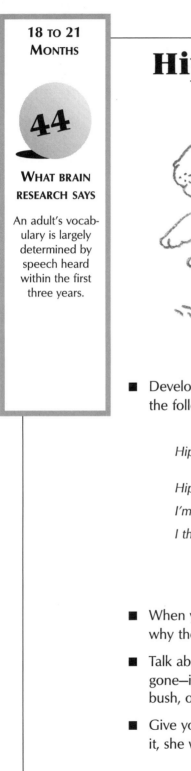

44

What brain research says

An adult's vocabulary is largely determined by speech heard within the first three years.

Hippety Hoppity

■ Develop your toddler's language skills by saying the following poem and doing the actions.

> *Hippety hoppity, hippety hoppity (jump like a bunny rabbit)*
>
> *Hippety hoppity, stop. (stop jumping)*
>
> *I'm so tired, I'm so tired. (yawn)*
>
> *I think I'm going to flop. (fall down on the ground)*
>
> Jackie Silberg

■ When you have stopped hopping, ask your child why the bunny rabbit was so tired.

■ Talk about the places the rabbit might have gone—into your yard, down the block, behind a bush, or into a garden.

■ Give your child the words and before you know it, she will be making up her own poem.

Animal Talk

WHAT BRAIN RESEARCH SAYS

Listening, watching, and giving words to experiences demonstrates interest in children and makes them feel like their thoughts and words are important.

- Toddlers love to make animal sounds and this game will help them associate sounds that go with different animals.

- It's best to start with two or three animals.

- Say the following.

    What does the doggie say?
    Woof, woof, woof.
    What does the kitty say?
    Meow, meow, meow.
    But the fishie, oh, the fishie
    Goes (move your mouth like a fish)

- The next time, start with a familiar animal, such as a dog or cat, then add a new animal and its sound. It is a good idea to look at pictures before you say the poem.

- Always end with the fish. A familiar end will give your child a feeling of security.

46

WHAT BRAIN RESEARCH SAYS

Expose your little one to a variety of sensory stimuli—colors, music, language, natural and mechanical sounds, touch, smell, taste—to ensure that, as an adult, she will have the most flexible brain power for learning.

Listen to the Sound

■ Take your toddler outside.

■ Help her become aware of the wonderful sounds of the outdoors.

■ Start listening for birds. When you hear a bird chatter, try to copy the sound and tell her that you are making the "birdie sound."

■ If you continue this, she will become aware of the sound and may try to duplicate it.

■ Add new sounds, such as the wind blowing or crickets chirping.

■ Listen for other sounds in your environment, such as car sounds, motorcycle sounds, and train sounds.

Important Accents

47

WHAT BRAIN RESEARCH SAYS

Scientists have found that young children develop a clear bias for words with first-syllable accents.

■ Saying favorite nursery rhymes is a wonderful way to develop language and pre-reading skills.

■ Try this game with rhymes that your toddler knows.

■ Say the rhyme, any rhyme, and put an accent on the first word of each line.

■ Any rhyme will do, but the following work well.

> *"London Bridge Is Falling Down"*
> *"Mary Had a Little Lamb"*
> *"Twinkle, Twinkle Little Star"*

■ Try some of your favorites.

48

**WHAT BRAIN
RESEARCH SAYS**

From the
moment a baby
is born, each and
every experience
builds the neural
connections that
guide develop-
ment.

Can You Find Me?

- Pick a favorite stuffed animal.

- Hide the animal while your toddler is watching.

- Say the following.

> *Where is bunny rabbit?*
> *Where could he be?*
> *Let's find him as quick as "one, two, three."*

- Go to the place that the bunny has been hidden and pull it out. Say, "Here is rabbit (or another stuffed animal), hooray!"

- Continue the game by hiding other toys. Always say the rhyme (changing the name of the stuffed animal) before you find the toy.

- Ask your toddler to hide a toy. Repeat the rhyme and let her find it.

- This game is a favorite of toddlers.

Oh, Hello

49

WHAT BRAIN RESEARCH SAYS

Research confirms that the way you interact with your child in the early years and the experiences you provide or encourage have a big impact on her emotional development, learning abilities, and ability to function in later life.

- Make a pop-up toy for your toddler. Make a small hole in the bottom of a paper cup. Put a straw through the hole.

- Attach a round piece of cardboard to one end of the straw. Draw a face on the cardboard.

- Show your little one how to pull the straw to make the face disappear and to push up on the straw to make the face appear.

- Chant the following.

    I know where you're hiding.
    I know where you're hiding.
    Hiding, hiding
    Oh, hello.

- On the words "oh, hello," push on the straw to make the face appear.

50

WHAT BRAIN
RESEARCH SAYS

By providing
warm, responsive
care, you
strengthen the
biological sys-
tems that help a
child handle her
emotions.

Food Fun

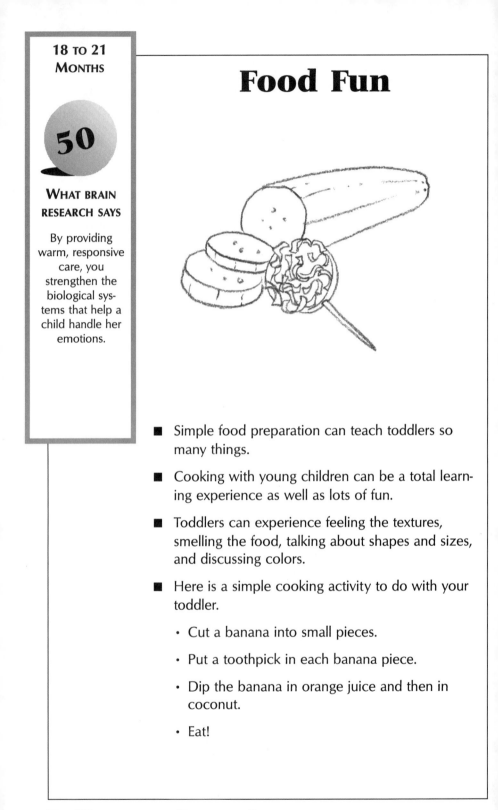

■ Simple food preparation can teach toddlers so many things.

■ Cooking with young children can be a total learning experience as well as lots of fun.

■ Toddlers can experience feeling the textures, smelling the food, talking about shapes and sizes, and discussing colors.

■ Here is a simple cooking activity to do with your toddler.

• Cut a banana into small pieces.

• Put a toothpick in each banana piece.

• Dip the banana in orange juice and then in coconut.

• Eat!

Clap Your Hands

WHAT BRAIN RESEARCH SAYS

Before a child can process language, he can process music. Early music experiences increase and enhance spatial-temporal reasoning and the learning of mathematical concepts.

■ Sing the following very slowly to the tune of "Row, Row, Your Boat."

> *Clap, clap, clap your hands*
>
> *Slowly every day. (clap your hands slowly)*
>
> *Merrily, merrily, merrily, merrily, (keep clapping)*
>
> *Then we shout, "Hooray." (jump up and down and shout "hooray" slowly)*

■ Sing this verse faster.

> *Clap, clap, clap your hands*
>
> *Faster every day. (clap your hands faster)*
>
> *Merrily, merrily, merrily, merrily,*
>
> *Then we shout, "Hooray."*
>
> *Jackie Silberg*

■ Sing this song with different actions. Always do the actions slowly at first, then speed them up. When children do fast and slow actions, they begin to internalize the concepts.

52

WHAT BRAIN RESEARCH SAYS

PET (Positron Emission Tomography) brain scans show increased activity in the brain's frontal cortex, where emotional development occurs, between the ages of six months and two years.

Rickety Rockety Rocking Horse

■ Pick up your child and hold him around the waist with his back on your chest.

■ Say the following and do the actions.

> *Rickety, rockety, rocking horse (walk slowly and move him up and down)*
>
> *Rickety, rockety, run. (run while holding him tightly)*
>
> *Rickety, rockey, rocking horse (walk slowly again)*
>
> *You're my honey bun. (hold him high in the air and kiss his neck)*

■ This kind of game is not only a lot of fun, but it also develops security and bonding with your child.

The Looking Game

WHAT BRAIN RESEARCH SAYS

A child's potential is determined in the early years—from the first moments of life to age three. These are the years when we create the promise of a child's future.

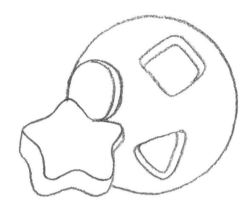

- Place a few familiar toys on each side of the room.

- Sit on the floor with your toddler.

- Show him how to lift his chin high in the air.

- Show him how to turn his head to one side and then the other side.

- Ask him to look at (name a toy) as he turns his head in either direction.

- Repeat places for him to look—look at the ceiling, look at the floor, etc.

WHAT BRAIN RESEARCH SAYS

Brain research underscores what educators have long argued: early social and emotional experiences are the seeds of human intelligence. Each child's neural circuits are carving highways in the brain where future learning will travel with ease.

Learning With Play

- Select several objects, such as a toothbrush, a spoon, or a cup, that your toddler is familiar with and uses on a regular basis.

- Set them on the floor.

- Sit in front of the objects.

- Pick up one object, such as the toothbrush, and pretend to brush your teeth.

- Pick up each object and pretend to use it.

- Ask your toddler to pick up one of the objects and show you how he would use it.

- This is a great game to develop your toddler's thinking skills and help him imagine other things to do with the same object, such as using a cup to drink from and for pouring.

Oh My Goodness, Oh My Gracious!

55

WHAT BRAIN RESEARCH SAYS

When children receive warm, responsive care, they are more likely to feel safe and secure and to be able to build attachments to others.

- To encourage a sense of security and safe feelings, say the following to your child.

> *Oh, my goodness,*
> *Oh, my gracious,*
> *Look who's here, look who's here.*
> *Oh, my goodness,*
> *Oh, my gracious,*
> *It's my favorite (child's name).*

- Hold your child close and give him a big hug.

- Repeat the poem again; when you hug your child, hold him high in the air and then bring him down for a big kiss.

- Try rocking him, slowly spinning him around, or any other loving motion.

- Your little one will absolutely love this!

**WHAT BRAIN
RESEARCH SAYS**

The size of a
two-year-old's
vocabulary is
strongly correlat-
ed with how
much an adult
talks to the child.
At 20 months,
children of chat-
ty mothers aver-
aged 131 more
words than chil-
dren of less talk-
ative mothers; at
two years, the
gap had more
than doubled to
295 words.

Dress-up

■ Playing dress-up is something toddlers love to do.
As you discuss the various clothes, you are
developing his language and giving him new
vocabulary.

■ Gather together all kinds of clothing—hats,
scarves, shoes, gloves, or whatever you think that
your toddler would enjoy.

■ Put on one of the hats and say, "How do you do,
Mr. (child's name)?"

■ Put on a glove and say, "Oh, this feels so
smooth."

■ Encourage your child to pick an article of clothing. Help him with words if he doesn't have his
own.

■ Soon, a conversation will develop and the language will flow.

Talk to the Animals

57

WHAT BRAIN RESEARCH SAYS

Scientists have shown that in stressful situations, children who have a secure attachment to a caregiver are more adaptive and produce less cortisol, a stress hormone that affects the metabolism, the immune system, and the brain.

■ Sit on the floor with your toddler. Pick a favorite stuffed animal or doll that your child likes to play with.

■ Carry on a conversation with the stuffed friend.

> *You: I took your cookie and ate it.*
>
> *Stuffed friend: Thank you for telling me.*
>
> *You: May I get you another cookie?*
>
> *Stuffed friend: Yes, thank you, I would like one. (pretend to eat a cookie)*
>
> *or*
>
> *You: I like to play dress-up with you.*
>
> *Stuffed friend: I like to wear the red scarf.*
>
> *You: Then we can pretend that it's wintertime.*
>
> *Stuffed friend: And it's snowing hard.*

■ Think up situations to act out with your toddler that can teach him about important events or situations in his life.

■ Acting out everyday situations helps the toddler understand them.

**WHAT BRAIN
RESEARCH SAYS**

From only a
handful of path-
ways at birth to
trillions of con-
nections by age
three, brain
growth in the
early years of life
is unparalleled,
according to sci-
entists.

Fly Little Bird

- Stand and face your toddler. Take his hands in yours.

- While holding hands, walk around in a circle and chant or say the following.

    Fly, little bird, through the window. (pretend to fly)
    Fly, little bird, through the door. (pretend to fly)
    Fly, little bird, through the window.
    Fly and touch the chair.

- On the words "fly and touch the chair," pretend to fly and touch a chair (or another object in the room). Ask your toddler to do the same thing.

- Fly and touch something different.

- This game teaches vocabulary in a very pleasant way.

Singing Names

WHAT BRAIN RESEARCH SAYS

The more words a child hears, the faster he learns language. The sound of words creates the neural circuitry that is necessary for children to develop language skills.

- Sit on the floor with your child.

- Name an object in the room that the child knows by chanting or saying, "I can see a teddy bear (or other familiar object)."

- Ask your child to touch the teddy bear.

- Continue by naming another object in the room. Each time you name an object, chant or say it in the sentence first, then ask your child to touch the object.

- This is a great vocabulary building game.

60

**WHAT BRAIN
RESEARCH SAYS**

A child's brain
grows through
experience and
attachment, two
critical compo-
nents necessary
to a child's
development.

Rickety Roo

- Put your toddler on your lap facing you. Hold him at the waist and move your knees up and down so that he can bounce.

- Say the following rhyme.

> *Rickety roo, Rickety ree*
>
> *Bouncing on your daddy's knee.*
>
> *Rickety roo, rickety row*
>
> *Stop the horsie*
>
> *Whoooaaa (pull your child close to you and give him a hug)*
>
> *Rickety roo, rickety rup*
>
> *Going up, up, up. (lift your child in the air)*
>
> *Rickety roo, rickety round*
>
> *Watch (child's name) going down! (support him under the arms while he falls between your knees)*
>
> Jackie Silberg

- Your child will want to do this over and over. It's the perfect way to develop attachment skills.

Sharing Music

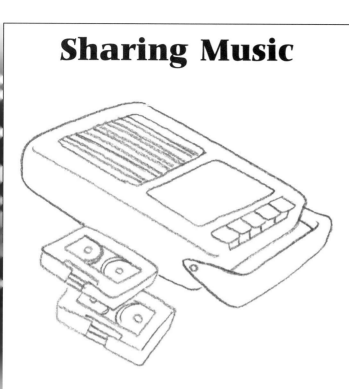

61

WHAT BRAIN RESEARCH SAYS

Musical experiences are vital to speech and motor development and sensory integration.

- Sharing music with your toddler will benefit your child's brain and give you both much pleasure.

- Play a variety of music (any kind that you and your child enjoy listening to) and respond to your child's movements. If he sways, you sway. If he jumps, you jump.

- Hold his hand and do different movements to the music. You can jump, slide, run, twirl, and tiptoe.

- Move freely to the music and let your toddler do the same. When he sees that you are enjoying the music, he will enjoy it too.

62

Sing in the Tub

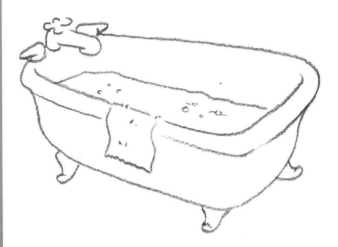

WHAT BRAIN RESEARCH SAYS

During the first three years of life, brain connections develop quickly in response to outside stimulation. When you snuggle a baby and sing to him in a rhythmic way, you are contributing to the growth of his brain.

- The time you spend bathing your child is a special bonding time for the two of you.

- Singing songs as you wash your child is a lot of fun and can teach language skills such as names for the parts of the body.

- As you wash your little one, sing about each part of the body that you wash to the tune of "Mary Had a Little Lamb."

    Now it's time to wash your toes

    Wash your toes, wash your toes.

    Now it's time to wash your toes

    Get them nice and clean.

- Sing the song again naming a different part of the body, such as legs, face, knees, ankles, wrists, and tummy.

Sink or Float

63

WHAT BRAIN RESEARCH SAYS

Problem solving helps make way for new learning. It causes new synapses to form by activating the chemicals that encourage new brain connections.

- Gather together several objects that will either sink or float.

- Suggestions include a sponge, soap, empty containers, full containers, floating toys, and a small toy that won't be damaged by the water.

- Put water into a bucket and start putting each item into the water.

- After each item use the words "sink" or "float" as appropriate.

- After you have tried each object individually, start again.

- This time, before you put an item into the water, ask your toddler, "Do you think it will float or sink?"

- Soon your toddler will be looking for other items to see if they will sink or float.

64

WHAT BRAIN RESEARCH SAYS

The more adults sing or play melodious and structured music to a child, the more the child's brain generates neural circuits and patterns.

Rhythm Fun

■ Sit on the floor with your child and give him a rhythm stick or a wooden spoon.

■ Try tapping a particular rhythm. For example, hit the stick two times and then stop. Count as you hit the stick, "One, two..."

■ If your little one cannot do this, hold his hand and hit the stick on the floor as you count.

■ Sing a favorite song and hit your stick on the floor to the rhythm of the song. Encourage him to copy you.

■ Once your child understands how to control the stick, give him directions and see if he can follow along.

  • Tap your stick fast.

  • Tap your stick slowly

  • Tap your stick loud.

  • Tap your stick softly.

Footsie Boom

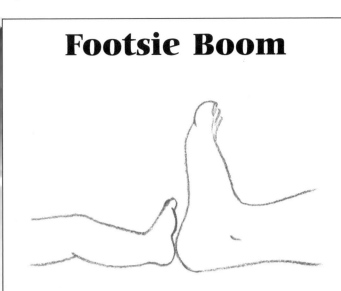

WHAT BRAIN RESEARCH SAYS

The emotional bonds you develop with your child impact his future learning abilities.

- Toddlers love to take off their shoes. This is a good barefoot game to play inside or outside.

- Both you and your child take off your shoes.

- Lie down on the floor with your feet touching your child's feet.

- Say the following, "One, two, three, and footsie boom!"

- On the words "footsie boom" lift your legs in the air and tap the soles of your child's feet with the soles of your feet.

- A nice variation is to let your child put a sticker on the bottom of each foot. Whatever the picture is on the sticker, change the words from "footsie boom" to "footsie dog" or "footsie baby," etc.

- What a fun way to develop a child's coordination!

66

Spin, Spin, Little Top

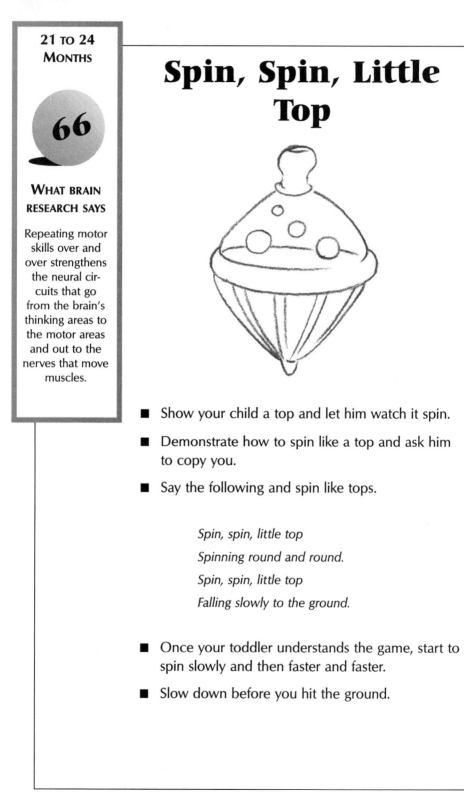

- Show your child a top and let him watch it spin.

- Demonstrate how to spin like a top and ask him to copy you.

- Say the following and spin like tops.

> *Spin, spin, little top*
> *Spinning round and round.*
> *Spin, spin, little top*
> *Falling slowly to the ground.*

- Once your toddler understands the game, start to spin slowly and then faster and faster.

- Slow down before you hit the ground.

Old MacDonald

WHAT BRAIN RESEARCH SAYS

A neurological scan of children who are singing nursery rhymes and doing counting games would show sections of their brains literally glowing with activity.

- A favorite song with young children is "Old MacDonald Had a Farm." They love to make the animal sounds.

- Try singing a new version of the song.

> *Old MacDonald had a cold, E, I, E, I, O*
> *And with his cold he had a cough, E, I, E, I, O*

- Add sounds you might make when you have a cold.

- Old MacDonald could also have a yard, a house, a candy store, etc. Changing the words develops vocabulary.

- For a challenge, sing this as a sequential song, repeating each animal mentioned at the end of each verse.

WHAT BRAIN
RESEARCH SAYS

Brain studies
indicate that par-
ents and educa-
tors have a gold-
en opportunity
to develop a
child's brain.
That means pro-
viding a rich
environment
without undue
academic stress.

Look at Yourself

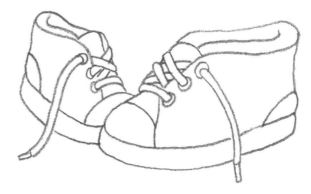

■ This is a wonderful game to help your child think about the different parts of her body and to enhance her observation skills.

■ Say to your two-year-old, "If you are wearing shoes, jump up and down."

■ Help your child by asking her, "Are you wearing shoes? Show me where they are."

■ Point to her shoes and ask her to jump up and down. You might need to demonstrate how to do the jumping.

■ Here are other ideas.

• If you are wearing socks, twist back and forth.

• If you are wearing a shirt, clap your hands.

• If you are wearing pants, shake your head up and down.

Whispering

69

WHAT BRAIN RESEARCH SAYS

Each time a child is stimulated to think, either new neural bridges are formed or pre-existing ones are strength-ened. The more neural bridges formed or strengthened, the more the intellect will be developed.

- Two-year-olds are fascinated by whispering and are very proud when they can do it.

- Whispering helps a child learn to modulate her voice, an important aspect of sound awareness. It also takes a lot of concentration.

- Whisper something to your two-year-old. Say, "Let's clap our hands."

- Ask your two-year-old to whisper something back to you.

- Keep whispering to each other until your two-year-old understands how to make her voice very soft.

Shake Your Fingers

**WHAT BRAIN
RESEARCH SAYS**

Positive early
experiences and
interactions
impact a child's
emotional devel-
opment.

■ Play this game with a doll or stuffed toy that has hands and feet.

■ Sit on the floor with your two-year-old and show her how to take the doll's arms and shake them up and down.

■ Give the toy to your child and let her try it.

■ Think of all the things that you can do with your stuffed animal.

■ Here are a few ideas.

  • Wave your hand.

  • Clap your hands.

  • Move your legs up and down.

  • Clap your feet together.

  • Throw a kiss.

■ Ask your two-year-old for her ideas.

Learning Rhymes

71

WHAT BRAIN RESEARCH SAYS

Memory is learning that sticks. When learning occurs, new synapses form and/or old synapses are strengthened.

- Two-year-olds are like sponges. They hear something once and are already beginning to memorize it, especially if it involves actions.

- An interesting way to say nursery rhymes is to accent the last word of each line and do an action at the same time. This will help her to memorize the rhyme.

- Here is an example. Remember to accent the last word.

> Hickory, dickory, DOCK (move your fingers in a climbing motion)
>
> The mouse ran up the CLOCK. (climb your fingers up again)
>
> The clock struck ONE, (hold up one finger)
>
> And down he RUN. (move the one finger down wards)
>
> Hickory, dickory, DOCK. (clap your hands on the word "dock")

WHAT BRAIN RESEARCH SAYS

A child's capacity to learn and thrive in a variety of settings depends on the interplay between nature (their genetic endowment) and nurture (the kind of care, stimulation, and teaching they receive).

Free Like the Wind

- It feels wonderful to hold a scarf in your hand as you move freely to music. It also gives you a sense of balance and control.

- Play some instrumental music as you and your child dance with scarves.

- Swoop the scarf high into the air and then low to the ground.

- Hold the scarf out as you turn in a circle.

- You and your child can each hold one end of the scarf and dance together.

- Whatever you do, your child will copy you.

- This is a very creative game and your child will want to play it again and again.

The Fruit Song

WHAT BRAIN RESEARCH SAYS

Scientists are finding that the kind of care young children receive has an even greater effect on brain development than most people previously suspected—a complicated mix of heredity and experience shapes brain development.

- Put three kinds of fruit on the table and name them.

- Let your child touch each one as you name it.

- Chant the following or sing to the tune of " Mary Had a Little Lamb."

> *(child's name) has a little apple,*
> *Little apple, little apple.*
> *(child's name) has a little apple*
> *And it's very good.*
>
> *(child's name) has a little grape....*
> *(child's name) has a little strawberry...*

- And finally:

> *(child's name) has a nice fruit salad*
> *Nice fruit salad, nice fruit salad.*
> *(child's name) has a nice fruit salad*
> *And she ate it up. Yum!*

74

What brain research says

The plasticity of the brain, its ability to re-wire itself, is what makes it so easy for children to learn language. The more words young children hear, the more connections their brains make.

The Fruit Story

- This is a good game to play after you have played the "The Fruit Song" game.

- Pick three or four fruits for your child to examine with you.

- One by one cut them open and talk about what's inside. Does it have seeds, a core, segments, etc.?

- Tell a story about the fruit, using your own words. The following is an example.

> *Once upon a time there was an apple that came to play with Billy. "Hi Billy, I'm glad to be here, but I am a bit lonely. Could we invite another fruit to come over and play?"*
>
> *"Okay," said Billy, "I'll call an orange."*
>
> *Billy dialed the phone and said, "Hello, orange. Would you like to come over to play?"*

- Let your child suggest whom to call next. With each new fruit, examine it, talk about it, and, of course, taste it.

A Butterfly Sandwich

WHAT BRAIN RESEARCH SAYS

"The brain is an association machine," says Dr. Larry Katz, a neurobiologist at Duke University. "The brain constantly looks to link things together—by sight, smell, sound, and space. Then it calls on those associations to make sense of the world."

■ Let your two-year-old help you make a sandwich.

■ Use one slice of bread and cut it diagonally.

■ Put on your child's favorite spread, such as butter or peanut butter, and then decorate it with colorful pieces of fruit, such as banana slices, cut-up grapes, raisins, and other fruits. Try to make it as colorful as you can.

■ Reverse the halves and you have butterfly.

■ Add vegetable sticks for the antenna.

■ After your child eats the butterfly, encourage her to pretend to be a butterfly and flit around the room.

76

Scientists have found that your relationship with your child affects her brain in many ways. By providing warm, responsive care, you strengthen the biological systems that help her handle her emotions.

Sweet Little Bunny

- Play this game using your two-year-old's favorite stuffed animal. Change the name of "bunny" to whatever stuffed animal that you are using.

- The game will develop her spatial concepts.

- Say the following poem and do the actions.

Sweet little bunny

Hopping on the ground. (hold the bunny and hop it up and down)

Sweet little bunny

Looking all around. (turn the bunny around)

Look up high (hold the bunny high in the air)

Look down low (bring the bunny down to the ground)

Run, run, run (run with bunny)

Oh, oh, oh,

Sweet little bunny

Where did you go? (hide the bunny behind your back)

Ring Around the Rosy Plus

What brain research says

All children learn. What they learn depends on what they have been exposed to. Because most of your child's brain development takes place after birth, you have many opportunities every day to contribute to her healthy brain development.

- Play the usual Ring Around the Rosy with your two-year-old. Hold hands, walk around in a circle, and sing the following words.

> *Ring around the rosy*
>
> *A pocketful of posy*
>
> *Ashes, ashes, we all fall down.*

- Fall down to the ground gently.

- Now change the action.

> *Ring around the rosy*
>
> *A pocket full of posy*
>
> *Ashes, ashes*
>
> *Turn around.*

- Other actions you can do are clap your hands; hop, hop, hop; jump up and down; or quack like a duck.

- This is a wonderful way to develop your child's spatial understanding.

78

When you express different emotions, you stimulate the brain. Emotions cause a release of chemicals that help the brain remember different feelings and the events that are related to those feelings.

Looking for Faces

- Sit with your two-year-old and find pictures of faces in magazines and books.

- Ask your child about the expression on the faces.

- Find a picture of a child's face that looks happy. Describe the emotion on the face of the picture and then ask your child to "make a happy face."

- Keep looking for happy face pictures.

- On another day look for different kinds of expressions. Excited, sad, and silly are good ones.

- Look for expressions that match the way your child is feeling that day.

- This game helps two-years-olds identify their feelings.

Mirror, Mirror

79

WHAT BRAIN RESEARCH SAYS

Children form a memory much more readily if the event has an emotional component to it.

- Sit on the floor with your child.

- Hold a mirror in your hand and say the following rhyme.

  Hello mirror, what do you see?
  I see a happy face looking at me.

- Smile and make a happy face. Speak in a happy-sounding voice.

- Give the mirror to your child and say the poem again. Ask her to make a happy face.

- Continue making different faces into the mirror. Demonstrate the face and then let your child copy you.

- Other emotions to express are sad, grouchy, sleepy, angry, silly, and surprised.

WHAT BRAIN RESEARCH SAYS

When a child is three, his brain is twice as active as that of a college student.

Building a House

- Sit on the floor with your two-year-old and lots of stackable blocks.

- Build a simple structure with three or four blocks.

- If your child does not start building something on his own, encourage him to copy you.

- If your child is interested in making more complicated buildings, let him take the lead.

- Add plastic animals and/or people to put in the structures your child builds.

Wind Up and Go

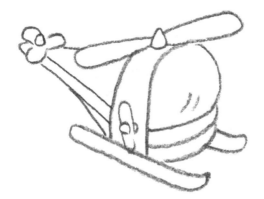

81

Upon birth, the brain has already begun to link billions of cells together—up to 15,000 connections (synapses) per cell. These synapses form the brain's physical "maps" that allow learning to take place.

■ This game develops your child's cooperation and language skills.

■ Sit on the floor with your toddler. Stretch your legs outward and try to get him to do the same.

■ With your feet touching each other's, make an enclosed area to play with a toy.

■ Turn the key of a wind-up toy and place it on the floor to move toward your child. As it moves, talk about the progress the toy is making. For example, say, "Here it comes" or "Watch out for the toy" or "Oops, it fell down."

■ If your toddler can wind up the toy by himself, let him do that and send it back to you.

■ If he needs your help, then wind it up but let him send it back to you.

Note: Some wind-up toys have small parts, so be sure to supervise this game closely and put the wind-up toy out of reach when you are done.

82

Attachments
between young
children and
their parents or
caregivers are
biologically
"wired" to forge
a close emotion-
al tie.

My Little Bird

■ Say the following poem and do the actions to enhance your child's feeling of security.

Here is a nest

All warm inside

Where my little bird

Can safely hide. (wrap your arms around your child and hold him closely)

Here is a nest

All hidden away

Where my little bird

Can sing and play. (give your child a toy)

Here is a nest

All cozy and deep

Where my little bird

Can go to sleep. (rock your little one gently and pretend to go to sleep)

Taking Turns

WHAT BRAIN RESEARCH SAYS

Pat-a-cake and peekaboo may look like innocent play, but the adult is also communicating a complex sets of rules about turn-taking and expectations. This kind of give-and-take is at the heart of all moral systems.

- Adults often get upset when their little one doesn't want to share. Sharing is a very difficult concept for toddlers and two-year-olds to understand.

- Taking turns is an easier way to understand the concept of sharing.

- Give your child a favorite toy and talk about the toy—how colorful it is, how nice it feels, etc.

- Take another toy for yourself and describe it.

- Play with your toy and ask your child to play with his.

- After a comfortable amount of time, give your toy to your child and ask him to let you play with his toy.

- If this doesn't work the first time, try it at another time.

84

WHAT BRAIN
RESEARCH SAYS

The human brain
is uniquely con-
structed to bene-
fit from warm,
loving experi-
ences and from
good teaching,
particularly dur-
ing the first years
of life.

The Smelly Game

- Select three different items that have a distinct odor. It's easiest to start with food and flowers. For example, interesting odors come from an orange, a pickle, and lilacs.

- Suggest to your child that you both pretend to be bears on a walk.

- Say, "Little bear, I smell something good."

- Pretend to pick an orange from a tree. Take off some of the skin and let your two-year-old smell it.

- Continue with the other two items that you have selected.

- Say, "Little Bear, let's sit in the grass and smell these things again."

- Finally, say to your little one, "Would you like to taste one of the things that we have smelled?"

I Know That!

85

What brain research says

Words have to come from a parent or other caregiver who talks with love and meaning in his voice, and not from television or radio.

- By this age, many two-year-olds know several nursery rhymes.

- Find pictures in magazines and catalogs that represent objects in the nursery rhymes that your two-year-old knows.

- Here are some examples.

  - A star for "Twinkle, Twinkle, Little Star"

  - A cake for "Pat-a-Cake"

  - A clock for "Hickory, Dickory, Dock"

  - A pail for "Jack and Jill"

  - A candlestick for "Jack Be Nimble"

  - A teapot for "I'm a Little Teapot"

- Show the picture to your child and say the words of the rhyme together.

- Glue the pictures on separate pieces of cardboard and put them into a can.

- Show your child how to pick a card and then say the rhyme together.

**WHAT BRAIN
RESEARCH SAYS**

Brain cells are
"turned on," new
connections are
made, and exist-
ing connections
are strengthened
by experiences
with stories.

Telling Stories

- Make up a story using your child's name. "Once upon a time there was a little boy named Mark."

- In the story, use two or three words that are repeated over and over. Encourage your child to say these words with you.

- For example, the story could be about "Mark" going to the park. Each time he sees something at the park that he recognizes, he says, "Hip hooray, fun today."

- Here is one idea.

  Once upon a time there was a little boy named Mark. Mark loved to go to the park and see all the wonderful things. When he saw the pretty flowers he said, "Hip hooray, fun today. " He sat down on the soft green grass and saw a little insect crawling by. He said, "Hip hooray, fun today."

- Shorten or lengthen a story, depending on your child's interests and attention span.

Magazine Fun

87

What brain research says

Experience counts in building vocabulary at a very young age. The size of a child's vocabulary is strongly related to how much a parent or caregiver talks to a child.

- Pick a magazine that is likely to have a variety of pictures of things that your child knows.

- Tape magazine pictures on index cards and turn this into a card game.

- Pick a card out of the pile.

- If you pick a picture of a cat, then your two-year-old should pretend to be a cat.

- This is an excellent game for developing imagination, language skills, and social skills.

88

Warm, everyday interactions like cuddling and singing will prepare children for learning throughout life.

Jack Be Nimble

■ Hold your child around the waist as you say the following popular nursery rhyme. Your child should be barefoot.

Jack be nimble

Jack be quick. (bounce your child while holding him around the waist)

Jack jumped over the candlestick. (bounce your child again)

Jack jumped up high. (hold your child high in the air)

Jack jumped down low. (come down to the ground)

Jack jumped over and burnt his toe. (say "oowww" and kiss your child's toe)

Fill in the Word

WHAT BRAIN RESEARCH SAYS

Talking to a child is the best way to develop his future language skills.

- Two-year-olds are developing language at a very fast rate.

- Make up a story with your child's name in it. Each time you come to his name, let him fill in the word.

- For example, "Once upon a time there was a little boy named _____ (your child's name). This little boy named _____ (let child fill in the word) went to the kitchen to eat his lunch."

- Add situations to the story that will encourage him to fill in more blanks. "_____ (Your child's name) opened the cabinet and took out some _____."

- Depending on your child, you can make the story simple or complicated, short or long.

- This game is an excellent way to develop both language skills and imagination.

90

WHAT BRAIN RESEARCH SAYS

Gross motor skills, fine motor skills, thinking skills—everything is learned by playing. When he finally gets it, his face lights up. That's what a child's play is all about—trying different things to find out what works and what doesn't.

Walkity Walkity Stop

■ Develop your two-year-old's coordination and large muscles by holding his hand as you walk and say the following.

Walkity, walkity, walkity, walkity
Walkity, walkity, stop.

■ Stop when you say "stop."

■ Change the movement from walking to hopping.

Hoppity, hoppity, hoppity, hoppity
Hoppity, hoppity, stop.

■ Stop again when you say "stop."

■ Keep changing the action, but always stop on the word "stop."

■ What you will find is that your child will know the exact time to stop.

Looking for Rocks

- Pick a nice day to look for rocks with your two-year-old.

- Talk about what you are going to do and take along a container to put the rocks in.

- Suggest to your two-year-old that you look for a certain kind of rock. "Let's find a small rock." "Let's find a smooth rock."

- You can look for rocks that are large, small, bumpy, smooth, prickly, white, brown, etc.

- When you are finished, bring the rocks home and wash them.

- Look at them closely and talk about where they might have come from.

- Let your two-year-old sort the rocks.

Note: If your child still puts things into his mouth, be sure you only collect rocks that do not pose a choking hazard.

WHAT BRAIN RESEARCH SAYS

New insights into brain development affirm what many parents and caregivers have known for years—that loving attachments between young children and adults, and stimulation that is positive and appropriate, really do make a difference in children's development.

WHAT BRAIN RESEARCH SAYS

At no other stage does the brain master so many activities with such ease.

Can You Do It Too?

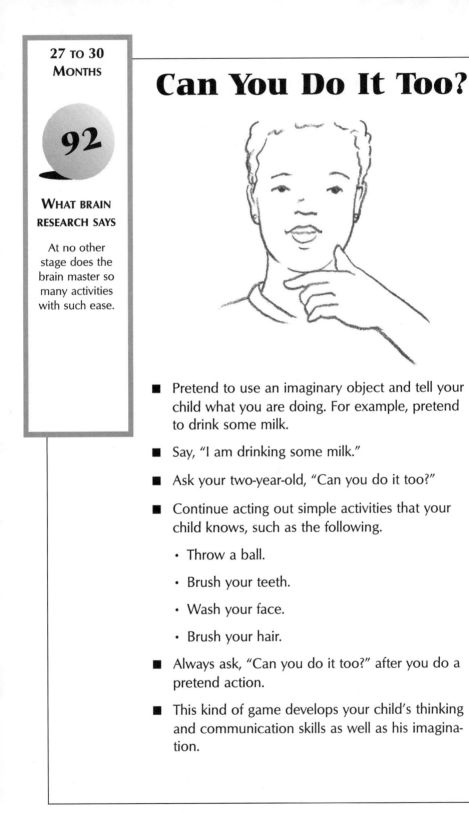

■ Pretend to use an imaginary object and tell your child what you are doing. For example, pretend to drink some milk.

■ Say, "I am drinking some milk."

■ Ask your two-year-old, "Can you do it too?"

■ Continue acting out simple activities that your child knows, such as the following.

- Throw a ball.

- Brush your teeth.

- Wash your face.

- Brush your hair.

■ Always ask, "Can you do it too?" after you do a pretend action.

■ This kind of game develops your child's thinking and communication skills as well as his imagination.

The Wheels on the Bus

WHAT BRAIN RESEARCH SAYS

Music optimizes brain development, enhances multiple intelligences, and facilitates bonding between adult and child.

- This song is a favorite of young children.

- If you don't know the melody, you can say the words or make up your own melody.

> *The wheels on the bus go round and round (roll your fists over one another)*
>
> *Round and round, round and round. (continue rolling fists)*
>
> *The wheels on the bus go round and round*
>
> *All through the town.*

- Continue with other verses.

> *The doors on the bus go open and shut...(open your hands and close them)*
>
> *The horn on the bus goes beep, beep, beep... (pretend to honk a horn)*
>
> *The kids on the bus go up and down...(move your body up and down)*

- And the all-time favorite verse

> *The baby on the bus goes waa, waa, waa... (pretend to cry)*

- Make up imaginative verses for the song.

> *Sheep on the bus go "baa, baa, baa"...*
>
> *Cows on the bus go "moo, moo, moo"...*
>
> *Dinosaurs on the bus go "grrr, grrr, grrr"...*

94

WHAT BRAIN
RESEARCH SAYS

The number of
brain connec-
tions increases
when a child
grows up in an
enriched envi-
ronment.

The Mice Game

- Say the following fingerplay and do the actions. Put your hands behind your back.

> *Five little mice went out to play (place hands in front of you)*
>
> *Looking for food along the way. (pretend to put the food in your mouth)*
>
> *Out came the pussy cat, sleek and fat (hold hands like claws)*
>
> *And four little mice went scampering back.*

- Repeat, subtracting the number of mice that scamper back.

- When you get to one little mouse and you say "out came the pussy cat sleek and fat," stop for a second, then say very quickly, "The mouse ran away, now what do you think of that!"

- Repeat the fingerplay and encourage your child to do the motions with you.

- Fingerplays are fun ways to develop a child's language and fine motor skills.

Bump Dity

WHAT BRAIN RESEARCH SAYS

Musical experiences integrate different skills simultaneously, therefore developing multiple brain connections.

- Take your two-year-old's favorite doll or stuffed animal.

- Ask him to touch the different parts of the doll's body. For example, say "Show me teddy's head" or "Show me teddy's toes."

- Take your index finger and chant, say, or sing the following as you tap the teddy bear on its head. Make up any melody.

    Take your finger and go like this
    Bump dity, bump dity, bump, bump, bump.

- Take your child's finger and repeat the words as you tap the teddy's head.

- Say the rhyme again as you tap the teddy's nose, or toe, or knee.

- The repeating of the word "bump" is a very good rhythmic exercise.

Repeating

**WHAT BRAIN
RESEARCH SAYS**

Children learn
language by
hearing words
over and over.
Language is a
critical skill since
it is a primary
communication
system.

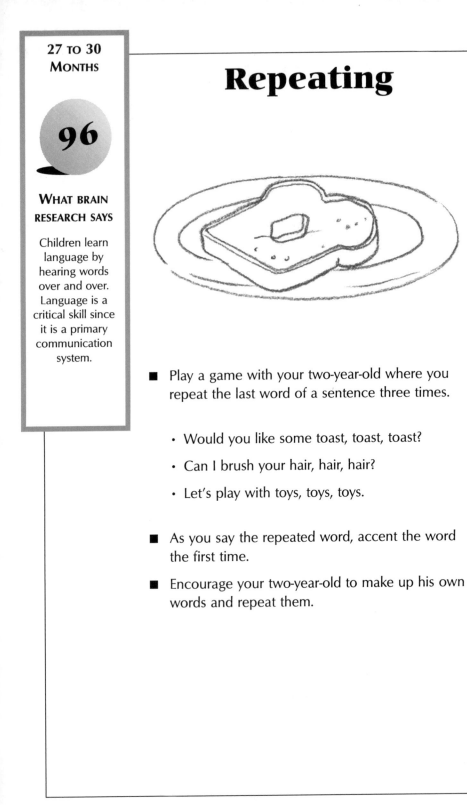

■ Play a game with your two-year-old where you
repeat the last word of a sentence three times.

   • Would you like some toast, toast, toast?

   • Can I brush your hair, hair, hair?

   • Let's play with toys, toys, toys.

■ As you say the repeated word, accent the word
the first time.

■ Encourage your two-year-old to make up his own
words and repeat them.

What Do You See?

97

WHAT BRAIN RESEARCH SAYS

During critical learning periods, or windows of opportunity, pathways grow that form the foundation for future skills.

- This is a very creative game that is good to play during a walk outside or a ride in the car.

- For example, if you are walking outside, ask your two-year-old what he sees. When he gives you an answer, stimulate his thinking by asking questions.

- If your child says that he sees a tree, here are some questions you could ask.

  - How big is the tree?

  - What color is it?

  - What do the leaves look like?

  - Where is the very top of the tree and the very bottom?

98

In the early years, children's brains form twice as many synapses as they will eventually need. If a child uses these synapses, they are reinforced and become part of his brain's permanent circuitry. If they are not used repeatedly, or often enough, they are eliminated.

Playing in Boxes

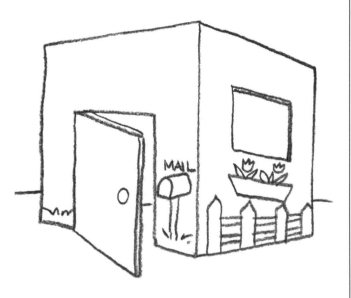

- Large boxes like the kind that appliances come in are wonderful toys.

- These boxes can become cars, houses, or whatever the imagination decides.

- Laundry baskets and other large containers are also wonderful toys.

- Boxes make wonderful places to hide treasures.

- Give your child a box and watch his creativity and imagination bloom.

Looking at Toys

The most rapid change in the brain occurs during the first three years of life when a child is bombarded with hundreds of new experiences. This is when the brain is most flexible and prepared to learn, building new connections and casting off others that aren't used.

- Look at your two-year-old's favorite toys. Try to find things that the toys have in common, such as wheels or colors or sounds they make.

- Pick two toys that are similar (two toys that make noise) and one that is different (one toy that does not make noise). Point out the two toys that are similar to your two-year-old. "Look Jenny, this toy makes a noise. Can you make a noise with that toy?"

- Keep playing and ask if another toy makes a noise.

100

**WHAT BRAIN
RESEARCH SAYS**

A strong bond to
a nurturing adult
can help a child
withstand the
ordinary stress of
daily life.

Puddle Watch

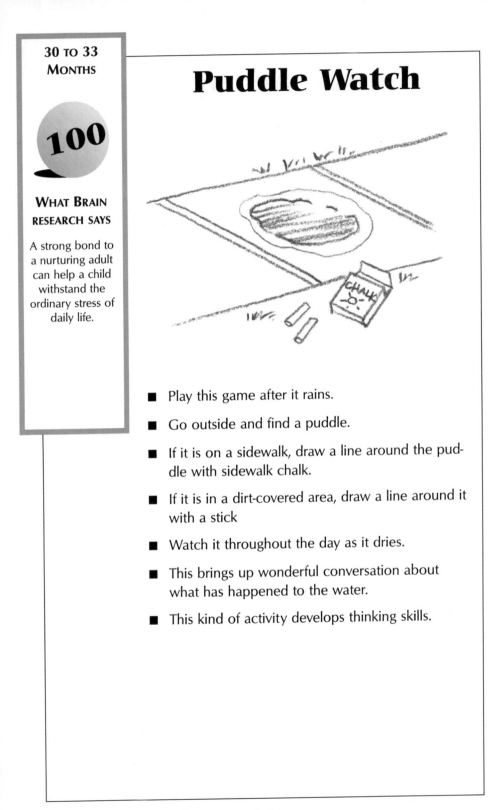

- Play this game after it rains.

- Go outside and find a puddle.

- If it is on a sidewalk, draw a line around the puddle with sidewalk chalk.

- If it is in a dirt-covered area, draw a line around it with a stick

- Watch it throughout the day as it dries.

- This brings up wonderful conversation about what has happened to the water.

- This kind of activity develops thinking skills.

Peanut Butter Sandwiches

- Most young children enjoy peanut butter and jelly sandwiches.

- To make spreading easier, use a spreader rather than a knife.

- Put out two pieces of bread.

- Let your child do as much as she can. Opening up the jars, putting the spreaders in the jars, and spreading the topping on the bread.

- Put peanut butter on one piece and jelly on the other.

- This will develop your child's self-confidence and her fine motor skills.

Note: As with any food activity, be aware of a child's food allergies.

WHAT BRAIN RESEARCH SAYS

During the first three years, a totally dependent child will build an incredibly complex new brain that will enable her to walk, talk, analyze, care, love, play, explore, and develop a unique emotional personality.

The Sequence Game

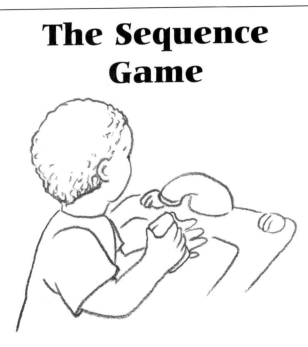

- Sequencing is an important pre-reading skill.

- Sequencing means doing a series of things in a certain order or pattern. It also means being able to repeat a pattern and to add onto a pattern.

- Helping your two-year-old learn to think in an orderly way will benefit her in the future.

- Self-care tasks, such as washing your hands, getting dressed, or brushing your teeth, are a good place to start thinking about sequencing.

- Chant the following.

  Now it's time to wash our hands.
  Now it's time to wash our hands.
  What comes next?

- Ask your child what will she do next. If she says, "Brush my teeth," then chant that.

- Add the new part each time.

When I Was...

WHAT BRAIN RESEARCH SAYS

One thing young children need for optimum brain development is a rich and responsive language environment in which they are exposed to a wide vocabulary.

■ Develop your two-year-old's language skills and imagination by chanting about different objects in the room and making up imaginative actions for them.

■ Chant or sing the following to the tune of "Mary Had a Little Lamb."

When I was a little chair
Little chair, little chair.
When I was a little chair
I could sit like this.

When I was a little train
Little train, little train.
When I was a little train
I could chug like this.

When I was a little ball
Little ball, little ball.
When I was a little ball
I could roll like this.

104

Here Comes Susie Moosey

- Say the following using your child's name and rhyming it. For example, "Here comes Bobby Dobby," "Here comes Aaron Baron," or "Here comes Jackie Wacky."

    Here comes Susie Moosey
    Walking down the street.
    She can walk a lot of ways
    Watch her little feet.

- Suggest an action for your two-year-old to do.

    Hop Susie Moosey
    Hop, hop, hop.
    You can hop down the street
    With your little feet. (hop with your child)

- Additional ideas are jump, run, tiptoe, slide, skate, and march.

- This game will develop her listening skills and her coordination.

Telling Stories

While children learn grammar more easily by hearing short sentences, children whose parents use many dependent clauses ("because" and "which") learn to use these in their speech earlier than the children of parents who do not.

- Tell a familiar story with repeated phrases.

- The following dialogue from "The Three Little Pigs" is a good example of repeated phrases.

    Wolf voice: Little pig, little pig, let me come in.

    Pig voice: Not by the hair on my chinny-chin-chin.

    Wolf voice: Then I'll huff and I'll puff and I'll blow your house in.

- Soon your two-year-old will be able to say the words with you.

- The following are additional stories, songs, or folktales with repeated phrases.

    "Goldilocks and the Three Bears"

    "The Three Billy Goats Gruff"

    Brown Bear, Brown Bear by Bill Martin Jr.

    "Miss Mary Mack"

    Caps for Sale by Esphyr Slobodkina

    "The Gingerbread Man"

**WHAT BRAIN
RESEARCH SAYS**

Causality is a key
component of
logic: If I smile,
Mommy smiles
back. A sense
that one thing
causes another
forms synapses
that will eventu-
ally support
more complex
concepts of
causality.

Favorite Poems

■ Two-year-olds love the rhyme, rhythm, and emotions that words conjure up, especially in poems.

■ The following are good poems to use with young
children.

"Hickory, Dickory, Dock"

"Hey, Diddle, Diddle"

"Jack and Jill"

"Humpty Dumpty"

"Twinkle, Twinkle, Little Star"

"Mary Had a Little Lamb"

"Jack Be Nimble"

"Patty Cake"

■ Say a poem with your two-year-old. Be dramatic
and try acting out the story.

■ The more dramatic and fun you make this, the
more your child will enjoy it. These kind of games
will remain with your child forever.

The Music Store

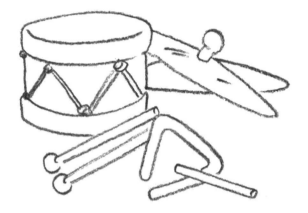

WHAT BRAIN RESEARCH SAYS

Hearing music or the sounds from instruments develops a child's innate potential to learn music when she gets older.

- Take your two-year-old to a store that sells musical instruments.

- If you have a friendly salesperson, he or she might let your child play on the piano.

- Show her two or three instruments. Again, someone in the store might demonstrate them.

- After your visit, talk about the things that you saw and heard.

- Play music that uses some of the instruments that you saw at the store. Point out the sounds as you listen together.

108

What brain research says

Neural plasticity, the brain's ability to adapt with experience, supports the idea that early stimulation sets the stage for how children will continue to learn and interact with others throughout life.

Singing Dinner

- The more you speak to your two-year-old, the more her brain will grow.

- Singing is another way to use language. It will help your child focus on the words and what they mean.

- Turn dinnertime into a song. Instead of speaking words like "Would you like some milk?" or "Here is a potato," sing or chant them.

- This is marvelous fun.

Again!

WHAT BRAIN RESEARCH SAYS

When the rhythm and melody of language become a part of a child's life, learning to read will be as natural as learning to walk and talk.

■ When two-year-olds like a poem, a book, or a song, they want to hear it again and again. Sometimes this is boring for the caregiver.

■ When this happens with a book, try asking the child to tell the story in her own words.

■ Read the story and let your two-year-old fill in some of the words. She probably has the story memorized by now.

■ Simple stories that your child can memorize are favorites at this age.

■ Reading stories will help your child have a longer attention span.

110

WHAT BRAIN RESEARCH SAYS

Children love to play. It comes naturally to them and is something they should be encouraged to do because it's essential to their development. Gross motor skills, fine motor skills, thinking skills—everything is learned through play.

Sorting Toys

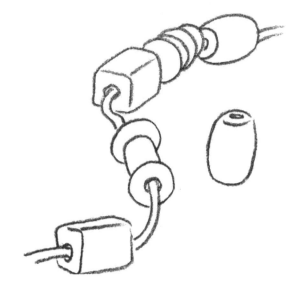

- Two-year-olds love their toys. The more you can play games that involve their toys, the more they will enjoy it.

- Sit on the floor with your two-year-old and put many toys in front of you.

- Start sorting by color. "Let's find all of the toys that have the color red and put them together." Continue sorting by color.

- You can sort by size, color, or characteristics (toys that have wheels, animal toys, etc.).

- Ask your child how she thinks the toys should be sorted. You and she will figure out many ways by looking at the toys.

- This game will develop your child's thinking skills.

Going on a Treasure Hunt

111

WHAT BRAIN RESEARCH SAYS

Although the brain is capable of learning throughout life, nothing will ever again match this most exuberant time of learning.

■ Hide three or four treasures outside.

■ Tie ribbons or crepe paper near the treasures, so that they will be easy to find.

■ Tell your child in advance what the treasures are, such as the following.

- Small toys hidden under some leaves

- Toys in a low branch of a tree

- Toys on the seat of a swing or at the end of a sliding board

■ Holding your two-year-old's hand, walk around the yard, and search for the treasures.

■ Finding the treasures is exciting for your child.

112

WHAT BRAIN RESEARCH SAYS

Movement is the only thing that integrates the right and left hemispheres of young learners.

Playing Hopscotch

- Draw a simple hopscotch grid on the sidewalk and number it up to five.

- Show your two-year-old how to throw a marker on one of the numbers. Use a pebble, a stick, or anything that is not too small and not sharp.

- Then ask her to hop to that number.

- You can also jump, run, or march to the designated number.

- This game develops coordination, balance, and counting skills.

The Puppy Game

The human brain develops most rapidly from birth to age six. Researchers universally agree that personality, attitudes, concepts of self, language, coping skills, and learning patterns are in place by age three.

- Designate an area of the room as the "doghouse" where the puppies play.

- Pretend to be the mommy or daddy dog with your two-year-old as the puppy.

- Ask your little puppy what his name is and call him by this name as you play the game.

- You can say, "Bow wow, woof woof, (puppy's name), let's hop over to the doghouse."

- Follow the direction and ask your child to do the same.

- Continue giving ideas for different things to do in the doghouse. Ask your child for his ideas.

- Other ideas include jump in the doghouse, march in the doghouse, crawl in the doghouse, and finally, eat in the doghouse. Pretend to chew on a bone, or maybe eat a real snack in the doghouse.

114

What brain research says

Every new move has to be repeated over and over to strengthen neural circuits.

Laundry Baskets

- Laundry baskets provide a great place to practice throwing skills.

- Experiment with throwing different objects like balls, wadded paper, and scarves into the basket.

- Each object will require a different kind of motor skill to get it into the basket.

- Place the basket close enough to your child so that he will be successful in getting the object into the basket.

- This is a great way to develop coordination.

Looking at the Moon

WHAT BRAIN RESEARCH SAYS

Experience and early attachments have a vital influence on determining brain structure. A child experiences the world through his senses, enabling the brain to create or modify connections.

- Look at the moon with your two-year-old. (Remember the moon sometimes rises during daytime.) Do it several days in a row and talk about the size and the shape each night.

- Draw a picture of the moon as you see it each night. It's fun to compare the shape and the size with other nights.

- Think of words to describe the moon, such as round, fat, long, skinny, etc.

- This is a great way to develop your child's observation skills.

Colored Ice

**WHAT BRAIN
RESEARCH SAYS**

The brain is a
self-organizing
organ. The con-
nections eagerly
await new expe-
riences that will
shape the brain
into the neural
networks for lan-
guage, reason-
ing, rational
thinking, prob-
lem solving, and
moral values.

- Make ice cubes using water mixed with food coloring that is non-toxic.

- Start with one color.

- Put the ice cubes in a dishpan or an unbreakable bin and play with the ice cubes. Use the name of the color with your conversation. "Please give me a blue ice cube."

- Use the ice cubes as blocks and try stacking them. Watching them melt is lots of fun and will bring up all kinds of conversation.

- Make another batch of ice cubes using two colors. This time compare the colors as you stack name them. When the ice cubes melt, you may have a different color. For example, if you are using red and yellow ice cubes, you will have orange liquid when they melt.

- This is perfect for a hot day!

Colorful Steps

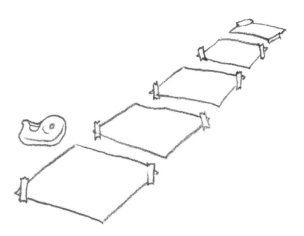

WHAT BRAIN RESEARCH SAYS

During critical brain growth periods long, thin fibers grow inside the brain, creating pathways that carry electrical impulses from cell to cell. The resulting network, which grows daily in the young brain, forms the neurological foundation upon which a child builds a lifetime of skills.

- Tape a construction paper path on a floor.

- Use two or three different colors in your path.

- Sing a favorite song as you and your two-year-old walk on the path. "Twinkle, Twinkle, Little Star" is a good song to use.

- Each time you stop singing, stop walking. If your child knows colors, ask him to name the color that you are standing on.

- Develop your child's spatial thinking by suggesting, "Let's walk over the paper," "Let's walk on the paper," or "Let's walk around the paper."

- You can also do other actions such as hopping, jumping, and tiptoeing.

118

What brain research says

Exposure to music rewires neural circuits that may also strengthen the circuits used in mathematics.

A Rhythm Game

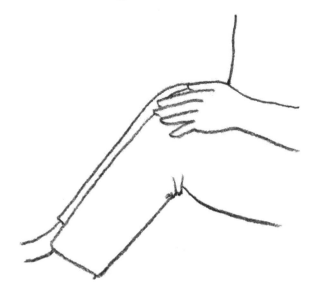

■ Say the following chant and do the actions.

> *One, two, three*
> *Touch your knee.*
> *One, two, three*
> *Knee, knee, knee.*

■ Repeat, changing the part of the body. For example, touch your arm or touch your toe.

■ The words do not have to rhyme.

■ Children learn an awareness of rhythm.

Where Is Jack?

119

WHAT BRAIN RESEARCH SAYS

Each young brain forms the neuronal and muscular connections required for sitting and crawling, walking and talking, at its own pace.

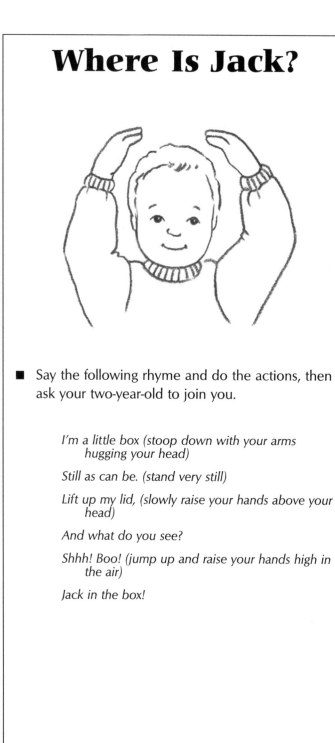

- Say the following rhyme and do the actions, then ask your two-year-old to join you.

I'm a little box (stoop down with your arms hugging your head)

Still as can be. (stand very still)

Lift up my lid, (slowly raise your hands above your head)

And what do you see?

Shhh! Boo! (jump up and raise your hands high in the air)

Jack in the box!

120

Muffin Man Rhymes

■ Sing the tune of "Do You know the Muffin Man?" using the following words.

> *Do you know the jo, jo, jo*
>
> *Ho, ho, ho*
>
> *Go, go, go*
>
> *Do you know the jo, jo, jo*
>
> *Ho, ho, go, go go, hey!*

■ As you sing the song, dance around and clap your hands on the word "hey."

■ Pick any three rhyming sounds to sing the song.

■ This helps your two-year-old learn about rhyming.

Bibbity, Boppity, Boo, Boo, Boo

**WHAT BRAIN
RESEARCH SAYS**

Nature and nurture are intertwined and inseparable. Nature provides an organ that craves experience and association. Nurture guides the process, ultimately deciding which pathways in the brain will be used and which will be ignored.

■ This simple little poem will make lots of connections in your two-year-old's brain.

■ Chant the following or make up any melody to this song and sing it to your child.

Bibity, bopity, boo, boo, boo
I love you.
Yes, I do.
Bibity, bopity, boo, boo, boo
You're my sweetie!

■ Try one of the following while you chant or sing the poem.

• Hold your child's hands and dance in a circle.

• Pick him up on the word "sweetie."

122

If the brain's visual and motor neurons are not trained between the ages of two and eleven, by adulthood the neurons are rarely "plastic" enough to be "rewired" for the job.

Funny Tricks

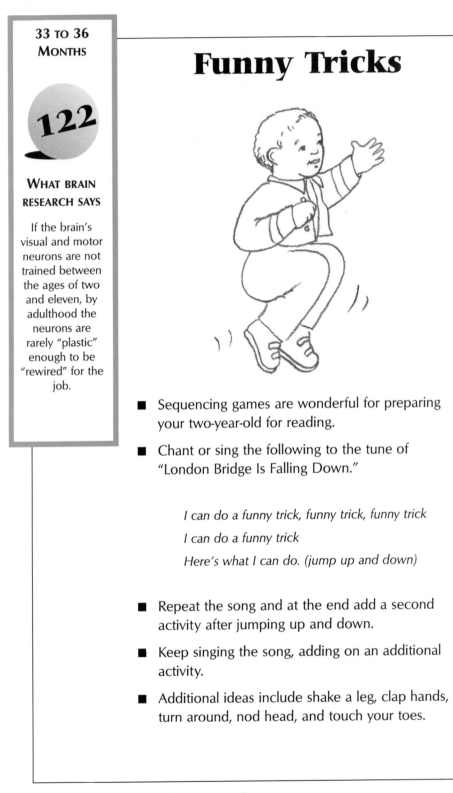

- Sequencing games are wonderful for preparing your two-year-old for reading.

- Chant or sing the following to the tune of "London Bridge Is Falling Down."

  I can do a funny trick, funny trick, funny trick
  I can do a funny trick
  Here's what I can do. (jump up and down)

- Repeat the song and at the end add a second activity after jumping up and down.

- Keep singing the song, adding on an additional activity.

- Additional ideas include shake a leg, clap hands, turn around, nod head, and touch your toes.

Musical Instruments

WHAT BRAIN RESEARCH SAYS

Dr. Mark Tramo, a neuroscientist at Harvard Medical School, reported that exposure to music "rewires" neural circuits. Like other circuits formed early in life, the ones for music will endure.

- Provide an assortment of rhythm instruments for two-year-olds to explore different kinds of sounds.

- Start with drums, sand blocks, triangle, and sticks.

- Drums: Hit it on the rim, then hit it in the middle. The sound will be higher and lower.

- Sand blocks: Rub them together to hear an interesting sound like a train.

- Triangle: Hit it at different places to produce higher and lower sounds.

- Sticks: Hit them on different surfaces to produce different sounds. Hitting a stick on the floor and then on a table will be fascinating to your child.

**WHAT BRAIN
RESEARCH SAYS**

In the course of
the first three
years, a totally
dependent child
will build an
incredibly com-
plex new brain
that will be the
beginning of a
new independ-
ent child.

Grocery Shopping

- Ask your child to help you prepare a grocery list.

- Take him to the supermarket and look for the items on the list.

- When you return home, let him help you put away the groceries and "read" the labels, box tops, and packages as you store them.

- If possible, make a recipe with the ingredients that you bought at the store.

- Praise the efforts of your two-year-old.

Let's Choose

125

WHAT BRAIN RESEARCH SAYS

The release of certain endorphins strengthens the functioning of brain connections. Positive, happy feelings cause the release of endorphins.

- Play this pretend game to help your two-year-old learn about choices.

- Sit on the floor with your child and put several stuffed animals on the floor with you.

- Talk to one of the animals. "Mr. Bear, would you like cereal or cheese today?" Ask your child to answer for Mr. Bear.

- Discuss the pros and cons of the choice.

- Pick up another animal and say, "Bunny Rabbit, are you going to play inside or outside today?"

- Here again is a good chance to discuss the answer.

- It is important for a child to feel good about the choices that he makes.

Bibliography

BOOKS

Caine, Geoffrey and Renate Caine. *Making Connections: Teaching and the Human Brain.* Chicago: Addison-Wesley, 1994. Fascinating information about brain research.

Carnegie Corporation of New York. *Starting Points: Meeting the Needs of Our Youngest Children.* New York: Carnegie Corporation, 1994. A task force of educators from throughout the country discusses many areas of developmental growth.

Gardner, Howard. *Frames of Mind: The Theory of Multiple Intelligences.* New York: Basic Books, 1983.

Healy, Jane M. *Your Child's Growing Mind.* New York: Doubleday, 1987. This excellent guide explains scientific theories of nervous system development. It also gives good practical information on how children develop language and mathematics.

Howard, Pierce J. *The Owners' Manual for the Brain: Everyday Application from Mind-Brain Research.* Austin, TX: Leornian Press, 1994.

Kotulak, Ronald. *Inside the Brain: Revolutionary Discoveries of How the Mind Works.* Kansas City, MO: Andrews and McMeel, 1996. Reinforces the importance of early experiences and the development of the brain.

Schiller, Pam. *Start Smart: Building Brain Power in the Early Years.* Beltsville, MD: Gryphon House, 1999. Simple, straightforward ways to boost brain power and increase a child's learning potential.

Shore, Rima. *Rethinking the Brain: New Insights into Early Development.* New York: Families and Work Institute, 1997. This book explains in lay terms the findings of recent brain research, and what the findings can mean for parents and teachers.

Silberg, Jackie. *125 Brain Games for Babies.* Beltsville, MD: Gryphon House, 1999. Interactive games to play with babies from birth to 12 months that "grow" the brain. Includes descriptions of how each game relates to the new brain research.

Sylwester, Robert. *A Celebration of Neurons: An Educator's Guide to the Human Brain.* Alexandria, VA: Association for Supervision and Curriculum Development, 1995. Emphasizes how schools produce an atmosphere for learning. Also describes the positive impact of social contacts and joyful feelings.

VIDEOS

10 Things Every Child Needs: The Crucial Role that Parents Play in Children's Brain Development. Chicago: McCormick Tribune Foundation, 435 North Michigan Ave., Suite 770, Chicago, IL 60611. Shows how the earliest interactions with children can influence brain development and promote social, emotional, and intellectual growth.

The All-Time Great Parent Test. Chicago: McCormick Tribune Foundation, 435 North Michigan Ave., Suite 770, Chicago, IL 60611. Features five recent winners of the Kohl/McCormick Early Childhood Teaching Awards who answer 12 important questions about child development.

Common Miracles: The New American Revolution in Learning. Peter Jennings and Bill Blakemore, ABC News Special, 60 minutes in length. Reveals how we can enable children to uncover their special strengths and become eager learners. A must-see if you care about children and education.

I am Your Child: The First Years Last Forever. www.iamyourchild.org A wonderful video about the new brain research and how parents and teachers can encourage a child's healthy development.

Your Child's Brain ABC -20/20. A wonderful overview of what we know about the brain today. Can be ordered from ABC.

ARTICLES

Adler, Eric. "Baby Talk: Babies Learn Language Early in Surprisingly Sophisticated Ways." *Kansas City Star* (November 12, 1995).

Begley, Sharon. "Mapping the Brain." *Newsweek* (April, 1992). Shows how different activities affect the various

Begley, Sharon. "How to Build a Baby's Brain." *Newsweek* (Spring/Summer 1997, Special Edition): 12-32. Describes how early experiences are essential to stimulate the newborn's brain.

Brownlee, Shannon. "Baby Talk." *U.S. News and World Report* (June 15, 1998): 48-55. Research shows that learning language is an extraordinary act of brain computation in infants.

Graziano, Amy, M. Peterson, and Gordon Shaw -" Enhanced Learning of Proportional Math Through Music Training and Spatial-temporal Training." *Neurological Research* (1999): 139-152. Forefront Publishing Group, 5 River Road #113, Wilton, CT 06897-4069.

Jabs, C. "Your Baby's Brain Power." *Working Mother Magazine* (November, 1996): 24-28. Helps parents understand the importance of interactions with young children.

Lally, Ronald J. "The Impact of Child Care Policies and Practices on Infant/Toddler Identity Formation." *Young Children* (November, 1995): 58-67.

Lorenz, Julia. "The Terrific Twos: Taking Care of Toddlers." *Early Childhood News Magazine* (November-December): 11-14.

Nash, Madeline "Fertile Minds. "*Time* (February 3, 1997): 48-63. A fascinating description of how the brain gets wired for vision, language, feelings, and movement for infants.

Newberger, Julee J. "New Brain Development Research: A Wonderful Opportunity to Build Public Support for Early Childhood Education." *Young Children* (May, 1997): 4-9.

Rauscher, Frances. "The Importance of Preschool Music: Enhancing Cognitive Development." NCJW (Fall, 1997): 16-17, 29-30. NCJW (National Council for Jewish Women) Journal, 53 West 23rd St., 6th Floor, NY, NY 10010. This article explains how music as an early experience contributes to the ability to reason abstractly, particularly in spatial domains.

Schiller, Pam. "Brain Development Research: Support and Challenges." *Child Care Information Exchange* (September, 1997)

Simmons, Tim and Ruth Sheehan. "Too Little to Late." *The News and Observer* Raleigh, NC (February16, 1997). Reinforces all that we are currently learning about the brain.

Trotter, Robert J. "The Play's the Thing." *Psychology Today* (January, 1987): 26-34. How face-to-face encounters help infants and toddlers develop their communication skills.

Viadero, Debra. "Brain Trust." *Education Week* (September 18, 1996).

Viadero, Debra. "Music on the Mind." *Education Week* (October, 1998): 25-27.

Zigler, Edward. Testimony by Zigler on the Policy Implications of Child Brain Development, U.S. Senate Labor and Human Resources Committee, Subcommittee on Children and Families, June 5, 1997. Available from American Psychological Association, APA Public Policy Office, 750 First Street NE, Washington, DC 20002-4242

WEBSITES

1ststep.com—various articles about brain research
ed.gov/pubs/html/child/videos.html—products available from the US Government
news-observer.com—online newspaper with articles about the brain
mbbnet.umn.edu/doric/brainscapes.html—University of Minnesota program for
    early education
rie.org—Magda Gerber and Tom Forrest, M.D., specialists in developmental and
    behavioral pediatrics have developed a unique philosophy and methodology
    for working with infants. RIE means Resources for Infant Educarers.
familiesandwork.org—Families and Work Institute

Index